Mastering the unexamined beliefs that
drive our financial lives

THE PROBLEM
WITH
MONEY?

IT'S NOT ABOUT THE MONEY!

JANE HONECK

Portland, Maine

Reversing Falls Press
50 Portland Pier, Portland, ME 04112
207-774-0882 • 207-773-2047 (fax)

First Edition

Publisher's Cataloging-In-Publication

Honeck, Jane.
    The problem with money? it's not about the money! : mastering
    the unexamined beliefs that drive our financial lives / Jane Honeck. --
    1st ed. -- Portland, ME : Reversing Falls Press, c2010.

        p. ; cm.

        ISBN: 978-0-9845020-0-4

        1. Finance, Personal. 2. Money--Psychological aspects. 3. Financial
        security. 4. Finance, Personal--Psychological aspects. 5. Finance,
        Personal--Decision making. I. Title.

    HG179 .H5966   2010 2010903971

    332.024--dc22   1005

Printed in the United States of America on acid-free paper.

Author Photo: Jo Moser
Cover and Book Design: Bacall Creative
Book Consultant: Ellen Reid
Illustrations: Lewis Agrell

To Janet O'Toole
business partner and friend
for your quiet strength and unconditional support

TABLE OF CONTENTS

Preface

FOR ONCE IN MY LIFE

O ver thirty years ago, after sitting for two-and-a-half-days with the toughest exam of my life, I became a Certified Public Accountant (CPA). The day I earned that title was the beginning of my professional life with money. Luckily, I hadn't listened to my father who had warned me, "No one will ever hire a woman accountant." Instead I had followed my dream to be a CPA and I began my career working under an innovative, bright, young tax partner with a Big Eight accounting firm who mentored me in tax and financial strategies.

While my left-brain knowledge and client relational skills continued to mature and develop, I soon grew impatient with the firm and its policies. (Ah, youth!) Following the suggestion of a close client, I left the Big Eight to start my own accounting firm. Fate followed me and a year later, my friend and associate, Janet, agreed to join me to help get my steadily growing workload done.

As the firm grew, I broadened my knowledge about personal finances and became a Personal Financial Specialist (PFS), the CPA's version of financial planner. With my financial comprehension expanding, I discovered that the thing I loved most about being a CPA was talking with my clients; numbers were fine, but clients were the real thing. I found that the topic of money and taxes automatically forged a close connection with my clients. This connection is where I found the passion for my work. I loved this *soft side* of money—helping my clients make financial decisions based on who they were and how they thought. I even had a physician client refer to me as his psycho-accountant—not because I was crazy, but because I helped him with that *other* side of money.

When my father died some years later, I embarked on a journey of personal discovery. With the workshops I attended and counselors who helped me, new doors opened to peace and understanding of me and my place in this world. As those doors opened, I began to feel a tug to do something more—something that would make a difference in this world. I used to say to friends and fellow journeyers that there had to be more because I didn't think St. Peter would greet me at heaven with a pat on the back saying, "Good job—you did a really nice tax return!" (At least I hoped it was St. Peter who met me!)

On this personal journey, I searched for fulfillment and a way to make a difference in this world. I began traveling parallel paths—one path expanding my accounting practice, the other expanding me personally. But I couldn't see any way for these two paths to converge. This time I wasn't impatient, just frustrated, as only a middle-aged woman can be. So I clung to both paths hoping to find a solution.

As the years flew by, I saw how my clients were stuck in their financial lives. They sought my advice for making all kinds of decisions, not only the usual ones you might expect, but also advice for major life decisions stymied by money constraints. I pointed out the pros and cons of their choices and instructed them in the mechanics of making necessary changes. And, I noticed the stuck places in their journeys mirrored my stuck places, so occasionally I would sneak in helpful suggestions that I learned on my own personal path.

At the same time, still searching for that ultimate fulfillment, I tried numerous side ventures: an innovative art program for children, light-hearted productions for television, gatherings for spiritual women, and even *Tick Tactic*, a Lyme disease first-aid kit. Nothing seemed to work until I said *yes* to a demanding and time-consuming program right in the middle of my busiest tax season.

I enrolled in the Empowerment Institute. Working with the methodology developed by Gail Straub and David Gershon over twenty-five years ago, I finally found the tools that brought my two paths together. I developed a Money Empowerment Workshop along with a Money Coaching Program and earned certification as an Empowerment Trainer. The financial programs I developed finally merged my two paths and freed my passion.

Thus was born *The Problem with Money?* Having worked with clients for more than thirty years, I knew that managing money was all about making choices. The Empowerment Institute helped me understand that our money choices aren't worth anything if we haven't examined the underlying beliefs and values. It's the beliefs about money that *lead* us to those choices. Without taking time to uncover those beliefs, we make our choices blindfolded.

How do I know this? I know from personal experience. One would think that a CPA/financial planner would have her money house in perfect order. After all, I have all the knowledge and talent to make good decisions—right? But left-brain power isn't the important piece of this puzzle. Just like you, I didn't know that unexamined beliefs were influencing the choices I made. I had that blindfold on too!

I remember getting my first job as an accountant at a whopping salary of $11,000 a year. I thought I had died and gone to heaven! Finally, I had some breathing room in my budget. Instead of having friends over for popcorn and beer, I could go out. I could buy a few trinkets, maybe even a new car. Life was good!

As my income grew, I thought about buying a home. I remember signing the papers on that first house hoping I could afford the $330 a month payment and laughing that it wouldn't be paid off until 2006. Oh, if only I still had that house and that payment!

Like others, I bought into the American dream. Bigger house, bigger car, bigger spending plan. In 2006 that mortgage wasn't paid off—oh no—that would be too easy. No, instead I had a newer, bigger (much bigger) mortgage with another thirty years to go. (If I only knew then what I know now!)

So you're not in this alone. My life with money mirrors your life with money. I'm not writing this book because I'm an expert in finances (well, maybe a little). I'm writing this book because I'm an expert, just like you, on *the problem with money*. I've lived it and I try to work the program every day because it sure is tempting to put that financial blindfold back on.

That's what this book is all about. *The Problem with Money?* is about removing those blindfolds and committing to leading financially conscious lives with fully examined beliefs so when we make our money choices we're making them with our eyes wide open.

My years as a CPA gave me the left-brain tools for how to handle money. My years as a woman searching for more in life gave me the right-brain tools for understanding why I operate the way I do. Together those years make it clear; this book isn't about me, you, or them—it is about us. We are in this together.

The Problem with Money? is about the beliefs and values that drive *our* money lives. It is about you and me and our friends and families. It's about our schools and churches and communities. It's about our nation and our world. It's about one great big *WE*.

We are going to explore the problem with money together. I'm going to lead the way because I have been digging into people's money beliefs (including my own) for a while. Ultimately, the journey is one we will be on together, because when one of us learns, we all gain—because we're all in this together!

A NOTE FROM JANE

The process you are about to undergo will change everything you've ever thought about money. So get ready and enjoy the ride. It may be bumpy at times; looking at money beliefs—or any beliefs for that matter—is not for the faint of heart. Be courageous, and don't take it too seriously. Life is too serious and everything you hear about money is way too serious. As I tell my clients, it's only money—you don't die or go to jail from money problems, so lighten up. There's much more to life than money!

So, try to have fun along the way. Anytime the process feels too heavy—take a break, talk to a friend, come back here to page 1 to remind yourself: *It's only money!* We're going to laugh at our foibles and our feeble attempts to change. Think of children taking those first, new steps—courageous for sure, but equally funny. (I used to think my kids looked like Herman Munster!) We're taking new steps to financially conscious lives. Let's laugh along the way.

And lastly, you don't have to do this alone. You may even want to do this with a friend or group of friends. Money matters combined with beliefs can be weighty topics—reach out and share this journey with others, try to make it fun. Remember, you're not alone in this—we all have money problems. Your friends will thank you for the invitation to join in.

During our time together, you'll be doing exercises to unearth your money beliefs. Have a journal or notebook at your side as you read this book. You'll use it to answer questions and to jot down things you notice as you start living a financially conscious life. Take lots of notes along the way. Being conscious with your money isn't automatic—the notes will remind you of where you've been and where you're going.

Good luck! Get ready for a fresh perspective that will take the burden off your shoulders once and for all!

Chapter I

WHAT'S THE BIG DEAL?

Choice. It's all about choice. Isn't that what life is? Should we eat this or that? Do we exercise today or not? Do we call a friend to help or do it alone? Every day we make choices that affect our lives. And sometimes we make deliberate choices we know we *shouldn't,* even though we are fully informed of the outcome.

I'm amazed at how I can start a diet in the morning, do fine all day, and at night hear that voice saying, *"There's ice cream in the freezer."* I ignore it—but it gets louder (no, it's not my husband). *"There's ice cream in the freezer."* I remind myself I *shouldn't* eat the ice cream; I want to be healthier and happier, and it feels so good to drop a few pounds—but you know the drill. The voice calls out even louder: *"There's ice cream in the freezer."* We all know what happens next!

3

It's the same with money. Anything and everything we do with our money is a choice. Spend or save? Buy this or that? Credit card or cash? Budget or not? The choices are never easy. But why? Sometimes we need more information, but other times we've dumped a whole lot of *should* on the choice.

Should we spend or invest? *Should* we buy this or that? *Should* we use a credit card or cash? *Must* we budget? (Oh wait, that's another one!) Should and must are good signs that something else is going on—that there is something more behind the decisions we make.

Money decisions all boil down to choice. And your choice is always correct if you are *conscious* of why you make your decisions. But unconscious choices get us into trouble. Unconscious choices wake us the next day, month, or year and make us say, "What have I done? How did I get here?" (Just like with the ice cream.)

When you ask those questions, you might blame and shame yourself. But you needn't. You don't wake up saying, "I wonder how I can screw up my finances today." We all start with good intentions. But those good intentions can't become reality because you are making financial decisions with a blindfold on!

So if you have good intentions—what chains you to your dysfunctional relationship with money? Why can't you make the changes you want to make? Why? Because you focus on the wrong problem—you deal with the mechanics of money management—what you *do* with your money.

But the problem with money is it's not about the money. That's right. *It's not about the money!* It's about the unexamined beliefs that drive our financial lives. These beliefs lead us to make money decisions with the wrong set of facts. And then we try to solve our problems with the wrong set of tools. It's like changing a tire on the wrong car with a curling iron instead of a tire iron! Your beliefs drive your financial bus, and you may be sitting behind the wheel with a blindfold on.

It's so clear during difficult economic times. Everywhere you turn—newspapers, radio, TV, the Internet—everything is about the current financial mess. It's as if nothing else is going on. They say we're in the midst of the worst economic crisis since the Great Depression, and it will be years before we climb out of this financial pit.

For the first time, financial stalwarts took a hit; some bailed out, some bankrupted, and some disappeared through merger or corporate death. Fannie Mae, Freddie Mac, Lehman Brothers, Merrill Lynch, AIG, General Motors, Chrysler, Wachovia, Washington Mutual—the list goes on and on. This time our government stepped in to stop the bleeding with programs like TARP, Home Buyer's Tax Credit, Cash for Clunkers, and more.

But this financial crisis didn't just affect them—it also affected us. Portfolios and retirement plans plummeted. Home values nose-dived until many owe more than their house is worth. Personal debt has increased to over two trillion dollars—almost $20,000 per household. And savings? What savings? Oops, we forgot to do that!

As individuals, businesses, and world citizens, we created a world based on our unexamined money beliefs. And because money is one of those taboo topics, we silently bought into a financial world we think we want. But if you really examine the beliefs shoring up this world, you will find they brought us lives we didn't fully intend.

What beliefs am I talking about? They're all around us. Think about the money messages you pick up every day. You receive messages from your family and society. Religion, education, and the media are full of hidden money messages. If you take the time, you can find money messages anywhere—even in those red and blue states.

As a child, you picked up subtle messages about money from your family. You learned that money is tough; there is never enough. Or that money is everything, and those that have nothing are lazy; they aren't even trying. On the other hand, you may have learned that having too much money was bad—what did *they* do to get it. You learned to live on less—or to live beyond your means. You learned that defaulting on loans is no big deal, or you lie awake at night worrying about your credit score.

We encounter conflicting messages from society and religion. If God provides all—where does work come in? Poverty goes hand in hand with piety. Abundance is ours if we just know how to access it right. To add to the confusion, over time, people misinterpret the messages. The lesson of "the love of money is the root of all evil" transforms to "money is the root of all evil." Come on—give us a break! How can we live in a world driven by money—without blame and shame—if we believe that?

Media and advertising messages affect our conscious and sub-conscious thoughts. We relate *priceless* images of uplifting, wonderful, non-monetary moments to spending until finally we believe that precious memories and spending are one and the same. *Don't leave home without it* instills fear, so we think the boogieman will catch us if money isn't close at hand. New products with new features tell us that we're nothing without the latest and greatest. And imbedded messages in movies and TV tell our subconscious, "Buy, buy, buy!"

Even our government jumps into this buying act. As the recession deepened, the government gave us stimulus checks, rebate programs, and tax credits to spend the country out of this economic disaster. The message sounds loud and clear—money and spending will save us all!

Through all this, the financial gurus confer left-brain money advice filled with messages of blame and shame. It's easy to get out of debt: just stop spending! You don't know your credit score? Stop being naïve! Choose the right investment or the right advisor and you'll have all you need. Take the nine steps to financial freedom—what are you waiting for? You're left feeling stupid and foolish for not doing what you *should* be able to do so easily!

We feel lost and frustrated. Everywhere we turn, we see problems with money. But the problem with money is *not* about the money! It's not about what we do with it; it's about the beliefs we bring to it. That's right, what we *bring* to it. You, me, us! It's about the beliefs that form the foundation of our financial world and drive our relationships with money.

Because we adopted these beliefs unconsciously, they're not even *genuine* beliefs. They don't represent our own needs and wants for a fulfilled life—they represent someone else's! We're destined to continue the same dysfunctional relationships with money over and over and over again. (Think of the movie *Ground Hog Day* with money!)

And because we're not aware of these beliefs, long-term, lasting financial change can't happen. Any attempt to modify our behavior is doomed to fail.

Haven't we all made promises to ourselves (and others) to spend less, charge less, and save more? How often have we followed through on those promises? And why haven't we? Is it because we're a bunch of liars?

Of course not! We make those promises with incomplete knowledge. But, when we are conscious of our underlying beliefs, we can follow through on our promises. When we are conscious of them, we can turn those beliefs around to reflect our real values and real self. And when they reflect your real values, your behavior will follow. You *will* make those changes, and you'll make them easily.

Because you'll be investigating your *own* beliefs, I'm not going to tell you what they *should* be. There is no right or wrong. No one, least of all me, can tell you that your beliefs should be something else—only you can choose what is best for you. This book will not point out what you have done wrong or what you could do better. (You all have moms and dads who already took care of that.) This book will not tell you how to handle money *right*. And it most definitely will not lay on blame and shame. Flush those down the toilet—blame and shame never helped one person with money (or anything else).

We won't be pointing our fingers at *them* either. We won't be blaming those who gave us bad advice or led us down the path to today's economic mess. You will take full responsibility for how and why you make financial decisions. You will become conscious of your money. This process involves you living your financial life fully awake and aware of the beliefs behind your financial choices. Because once you are wholly conscious, you will lead your own financial life—not someone else's. After all, it's *your* money!

The examples and stories in this book will show you how beliefs affect your money in unconscious and unintentional ways. They will help you find the beliefs behind your own financial behaviors. Lastly, they will show you how money beliefs surface in other areas of your life.

Once you find your own beliefs, you will examine them and choose whether you want them or not. You may decide the consequences of those beliefs are exactly what you desire. Or you may decide they don't reflect your true intentions at all. Only you can decide what is best for you. But when you do—then, and only then—can you make conscious choices.

I uncovered the truth about unexamined beliefs during my years of working with individuals, families, and businesses. I worked with people like John and Sharon, a young couple who came to me for help in cleaning up their overwhelming credit card debt. I taught them about credit card debt and interest rates and gave them left-brain tools for paying off this debt. I reviewed their budget and helped them make wise spending decisions. They left my office fully committed to making the changes necessary to get rid of their debt.

Five or so years later, John and Sharon came back—and not with tons of excess dollars to invest. No, they returned with the same old problem, only this time the debt had grown along with their increasing incomes. Now they were back with piles of *should* and buckets of *shame* for not following through.

I knew then that the problem with money was not about the money. I knew just talking about the mechanics of finance wasn't enough. I knew using only left-brain solutions wasn't going to solve money problems. I knew something lurked behind the scenes of their money life. No change could possibly occur until they uncovered the money beliefs trapping them.

Your journey begins with understanding the issue. When you make choices based on unexamined beliefs, you aren't in the driver's seat—your unconscious beliefs are. If you want freedom to make your own real choices based on conscious beliefs, you need to uncover those beliefs. Once you find them, you'll see how they affect not only money but all aspects of your life. You'll examine them to find the truth. Then, and only then, can you transform them into conscious beliefs—*your* beliefs, beliefs you can really live by and follow.

HUSH MONEY

Why do we end up with these unexamined beliefs—why are they unconscious? Because no one talks openly about money! Money, like sex, is a forbidden topic. Both are laden with unexamined beliefs and fears. The subtle nuances aren't openly discussed or debated, so we internalize the messages we pick up, turn them into beliefs and fears, and make them our own. And because they aren't really *our* truths, when we can't live by them, we cover them with loads of blame and shame.

As a child, you learned not to talk about money, to avoid the topic entirely. Remember your mom's horrified look and your dad's chuckle when you asked Aunt Julie what she did to get all that money? In subtle and not-so-subtle ways, you learned to avoid the topic of money. A roll of the eyes, an embarrassed cough, or shocked look met your questions. You received the message clearly—money talk is off limits!

Back in second grade and before women's lib, my teacher Mrs. Caldwell asked me to fill out a questionnaire about family income. "How much does your father earn?" I remember having absolutely no clue. Was it $200? $2,000? $20,000? If we ever talked about this at the dinner table, I must have been sleeping!

By then, I had already picked up conflicting messages about our money situation. Dad was a Chevrolet car dealer, so he always drove shiny, new cars—that must mean we had money, right? But that same shiny, new car could be gone in a minute if someone wanted to buy it. Did that mean we needed money? We loved that car and now it was gone! What was it—what was the truth? When I asked my parents to fill in the blanks for me, they told me I didn't need to know, it wasn't important, and it was nobody's business. It was clear—we would not be talking about money!

The silence you learned from your parents is easily passed on. I remember when my son, Kilian, was a five-year-old and asking to go to McDonald's for lunch. I explained we really didn't have the money to go that day—we needed to watch our dollars. Later that afternoon in the produce department at the grocery store, he turned to me with tears in his beautiful, blue eyes and asked, "Do we have enough money for apples?" Clearly, he didn't have complete information!

Not talking about money leaves us in confusion. We wonder, *How much is enough? How much do I deserve? Why don't I ever have enough? Am I good enough, smart enough, responsible enough? Why don't I know?*

The silence doesn't give you the opportunity to sort out, question, or understand the messages you gathered. Instead, you try to figure it out based on misinformation, prejudices, and idiosyncrasies. You turn the messages into unconscious beliefs that burrow deep into your unconscious because you can't share or talk about them. And so, you begin your money life financially unconscious, filled with someone else's beliefs.

MONEY, MONEY, POWER MONEY

Not talking about money isn't the only thing fueling our confusion. Unexamined individual and societal beliefs have so influenced our values that we now give money more power than it deserves. Money controls more and more in our world. We find ourselves in crisis because the power we believed money had isn't enough to keep our world going. Today's challenging times lead us to think again about the almighty dollar and the power we give it.

What is the the real power of money, what is its value? The only value money possesses is what we humans give it. Money certainly didn't come into this world with power. Money is man-made, and we furnished it with power by using it to assign value to things in our world. Of course, there is need for some form of currency to operate our world, but we have lost sight of the initial purpose of money. Instead of retaining economic power for the exchange of goods and services, money's power has transformed so that just the mere possession of money grants the possessor worth and value.

We endowed money with this power, and this is reflected everywhere in our society. Education isn't an equal opportunity any longer with poorer communities falling short of the opportunities afforded wealthier communities. And even within those wealthier schools, *poorer* students fall short of the more affluent students.

The value of your profession is determined not by what you do but rather by how much you earn. The powerful dollar establishes that our society prizes being a wealthy lawyer or superstar athlete more than being a teacher or social worker.

Potential loss of money taints religious decision-making, and powerful new religious groups spring up with large numbers of followers. But, sometimes on closer inspection, we find the beliefs and values working behind the scenes weren't shaped by God but rather by the almighty dollar.

Raising the most campaign funds wins elections. If you don't have enough money, you can't enter politics. All too often, politicians lose their offices because they have been enticed by the power of money; they sold their beliefs and values to the highest bidder.

Unfortunately, money has become the symbol for what is important in life. The power we assigned to money has distorted the real values of life. Behind that distortion of power are unexamined money beliefs.

But what do you really believe? Isn't what you believe important? Can you have an opinion based on *your* money beliefs—not someone else's?

MONEY, MONEY EVERYWHERE

Because we use money to assign value and power, our society arranges itself for the accumulation of money. Because of this, the concept of *enough* becomes bottomless. We see individuals, companies, and governments solely focused on the bottom line and amassing great fortunes. Financial markets develop schemes not for the strength and value they bestow to the general public but because these products increase the company's net worth. Unfortunately, decisions made solely from the perspective of financial power overlook the human factor.

Focusing on accumulating powerful dollars causes the gap between those who have and those who have not to widen until it is nearly impossible to see across the great divide; we begin to think we're from different planets. Both sides' unexamined beliefs make it unfeasible for either side to bridge the gap. The two sides hold onto opposing beliefs and can't even begin to understand the other side (nor do they want to).

With the widening of this gap, misleading, unconscious beliefs grow stronger until each side sees them as truths that will never change. One side believes that nothing good accompanies money, while across the gap others think if one doesn't have money, one is no good. One side believes people did something *bad to* obtain money, and the other side thinks if people just tried *harder*, they wouldn't be in that financial mess.

The gap between the *haves* and *have-nots* continues to widen—and is based on baseless *truths* that cause us all to choose sides. Just watch political commentators with their red and blue maps to see how divided we are. Unexamined money beliefs are behind this great segregation. They may be disguised as other issues, but look closely and you'll see money at their root.

Unfortunately, these money beliefs not only affect our finances—they influence other parts of our lives. Current divorce statistics tell us that 50 percent of all American marriages end in divorce, and one of the biggest stressors is money. And guess what? Behind that money stress lies unexamined beliefs—only now, they are amplified and result in miscommunication every day. It doesn't take a rocket scientist to realize that miscommunication combined with financial stress quickly leads to divorce!

Our schools and children are at risk because budget constraints cut educational programs every year. Any discussions about the efficacy of these programs and their long-term benefits are lost in the battle for dollars and cents. Our public schools offer less robust programs, reducing our children's preparedness for the real world. On top of that, those who *have* choose to educate their children in private schools, and once again, the gap continues to widen.

Traditional religions suffer from unexamined money beliefs. Churches that were the strength of many communities close because they no longer have the members needed to support the financial structure of the church or because bad decisions were made to cover up issues that seemed too costly to deal with at the time. We no longer can find solace in traditional places. And with their demise comes the loss of community and its intangible value in our lives.

Every day, important city, state, and national community programs close due to finances. Programs that help build strong families and robust communities fall victim to lack of funding. And as we lose these programs, once again we lose community building and their related intangible assets.

Behind all of these losses are decisions based on money beliefs—beliefs based on the power we give money, power originating in unexamined, unconscious beliefs buried deep inside because we never learned to talk about them.

All of this is why I know that the problem with money is not about the money!

MONEY ON THE MIND

Because we hold these unconscious money beliefs and because we imbue money with this inordinate amount of power, our money problems directly influence most other parts of our lives. It's no surprise that the pursuit of money drives our everyday actions.

We work longer and longer hours to support our lifestyles—lifestyles that we inadvertently bought into. Our cars and homes have grown bigger and bigger. Back in the seventies, we shunned big cars and prided ourselves on small, energy-efficient automobiles—even exaggerating a bit in order to be the owner of the most fuel-efficient, cost-effective vehicle. Now advertising and *looking good* sell us gas-guzzling status symbols, and we unconsciously believe that the size of our wheels shows the world our *power*.

McMansions exist everywhere. Young couples sacrifice everything to gain these symbols of power and success. Carole, an interior designer I know, laments how she tries to help young couples decorate their big, beautiful houses devoid of furniture. They have no money remaining to turn their houses into homes. Now with the economic crisis, these homes act as abandoned symbols of unfulfilled dreams and promises.

At earlier and earlier ages, we ask our children to mirror this *powerful* lifestyle. With designer clothing from birth and the *right* obligatory classes, they don't have time to be just children. Before they know what hit them, they are on that path of unexamined money beliefs. They need to gain entrance into the right nursery school to be accepted into the right elementary school, middle school, high school, and college so they can find their place in this world. They haven't even figured out potty training, and we've already decided how money and its power will affect their lives.

The unconscious beliefs we absorbed told us that to be a good parent we must provide the best of everything for our families. So our children learn to expect it. Now scores of entitled youth find it difficult to make it in the world. We lift up a lifestyle for them to strive for, but we haven't given them sound financial beliefs to help them get there. Consequently, they find it more and more difficult to operate in the society we created for *them*. Who do we blame? Them, of course—just like our parents blamed us.

Our unconscious, unexamined money beliefs create foundations we didn't plan for or intentionally build. Because we don't talk about money, we fashioned our lives around beliefs that don't reflect who we are or what we believe. These unconscious beliefs give money more power than it deserves and motivate us to live our lives in unconscious and dysfunctional ways.

Only by discovering these beliefs and bringing them to light will you have a chance to change your financial journey and your life.

Chapter II

COME OUT, COME OUT

WHEREVER YOU ARE!

You've now discovered that unconscious, unexamined money beliefs have run your life (not just on a personal level but also on a societal level). Because people don't openly talk about money (at least not in depth), the power of money created a world you may not fully understand or want.

In these challenging times, you may face the real possibility that there's not enough money for the *things* in your world and that, ultimately, money won't be enough to fulfill your life. You may feel panicked. And why shouldn't you? You know the financial world has shifted. Like it or not, your financial life, along with your beliefs, must shift too.

But how do you begin the process of shifting those unconscious money beliefs? You must embark on an archaeological dig—a dig into your inner life with money. You must find the unconscious, unexamined beliefs that have been running your life and bring them to light. Once you are aware of these beliefs, you can discover the truths about them. Do they support your way of thinking, feeling, and living? Do they represent who you really want to be—who you really are? Are they your beliefs or someone else's? Do you want them or not?

Ready or not, here we go!

MEMORIES OF MONEY

The search begins with your earliest memories of money. You already know my first memory—the second-grade income questionnaire. It must have been important to me because I still remember it. I also remember an incident when my oldest son John was just six. I'm not sure if it is *his* first financial memory, but I do know it affected his life with money:

> John and I were checking out at Sears in the mall. As I pulled out my credit card and handed it to the clerk, I noticed John watching closely. He asked me, "What's that? Aren't you going to pay?" I explained how the store took the credit card information and would send me a bill to pay in about a month. I saw the wheels spinning in his little red head and he said, "Couldn't you pay for the bill with another credit card? Then pay for that bill with another card? And then another card and another—and never have to pay?" At six, he had already figured out the American way! And guess what his first, real job was? Selling credit cards!

We each have memories about our first encounter with money. Was it your allowance? Was it receiving gifts? What was it? Why did your first memory stick in your mind?

et's begin your archeological dig by thinking back to that earliest memory. Like me, you may be able to go directly to that memory. Or you may need some time to remember; if that sounds like you, just close your eyes for a moment. Take a few deep breaths and wait for something to reveal itself. Don't judge what comes up—even the most inconsequential thing often reveals the most information. Give yourself time to connect with that memory.

Once you find the memory, use the journal to take notes as you self-reflect. Write down the story as you would have told it if you had been encouraged to talk about the incident. Write it from a child's viewpoint; don't use your adult interpretation. Include as much detail as possible to help you access your original feelings and thoughts.

How old were you?

Where were you?

Who was with you?

What were you feeling—anxiety or fear? Anticipation or happiness?—What?

After you've written the story in detail, list any beliefs that might have developed from that incident. For example, do you believe that money buys happiness? That money is limitless? Or is money a source of fear and anxiety?

 Record those beliefs in the Unexamined Beliefs log at the end of this book.

OUR FAMILIES

Your earliest money beliefs may have come from your family. How your family modeled money directly affects your relationship with money. Even though your family may not have spoken openly about money, their actions and energy spoke louder than words. Whether the message was one you followed or ignored, it still drives your money life.

Mary had a father who always told her, "Without money, I am nothing!" She lived in constant fear of never having enough and becoming a bag lady. She prided herself on extreme frugality although she really didn't need to be so careful. More importantly, she pegged her own self-worth to money. She *knew* that people in her life were only there because of the money she had—not because of who she was. Unfortunately, an unexamined money belief handed down from her father stripped her of her own self-worth!

Earlier generations pass down family beliefs to the following generations. And as the beliefs are passed down, your parents had the choice to accept or reject them—and so do you.

One father called himself a "child of the depression" and prided himself on his frugal decisions, such as buying shoes for $4.99 or ordering the most stripped-down basic car available. One of his sons said he seemed to have picked up his father's manner of handling money because he too was quite frugal. His brother, on the other hand, called himself a "grandchild of the depression" as he drove away in his Jaguar! One son accepted the belief, but the other rejected it.

Whether your family consisted of the proverbial two-parent, two-children, and one-dog household or some other configuration, your money beliefs originated there. Because you didn't talk about them in depth, those unexamined money beliefs still drive your financial life. Whether you accepted or rejected the beliefs doesn't matter—they still influence you.

Using your journal, write about your family and money. If you think you have nothing to write about, think again. Not having anything to write about is meaningful—maybe even more consequential than having much to say. Just write what occurs to you with no censorship allowed. You want to find those unexamined beliefs as they first come up—not as you would like to reinterpret them.

Answer these questions to help discover family patterns:

Did your parents talk about money?

Was there plenty of money or never enough?

Was money important or not?

How did your family finances compare to other friends and relatives?

What was the feeling around money—any anxiety or fear—comfort or peace—or anything else?

After you spend time answering these questions, write the most important story about money in your family. Use your imagination to investigate, and remember no judgments are allowed.

What did you, as part of that family, learn about money? Did your family value money, hoard money, or spend it frivolously? What was your family's unique lesson about money? What unexamined beliefs were passed on to you?

 Add those beliefs to the Unexamined Beliefs log in the back.

RELATE THIS

The significant relationships in your life also reveal important money beliefs. These beliefs surface when you look at joint financial dealings with your spouse, significant other, or even siblings and friends.

> I worked with a young couple whose finances were a mess. Expecting their second child, Laurie and Joel were concerned they might not be able to make it through another maternity leave. In the process of getting to know them, I found they kept their finances (and money decisions) totally separate. Our work uncovered that Laurie believed she was a fully independent woman because she didn't share her finances with anyone. Joel believed he couldn't trust anyone but himself with his money: He *knew* that he was the only one responsible enough to make the right decisions. These two unspoken beliefs wreaked havoc with their finances. More importantly, until Laurie and Joel uncovered and openly discussed these issues, they only added stress to an already overwhelmed marriage.

I have worked with many divorced men and women who soon discover that a huge part of their dysfunctional ex-marriages revolved around money. Their financial beliefs contributed to an imbalance of power, and a true partnership never existed between them. And sometimes divorce freed them to participate fully in their own financial decisions and their lives.

> Gloria found herself divorced after forty-two years of marriage. Devastated, she couldn't imagine how her life would continue. Instead, Gloria discovered she grew stronger in her overall life as she worked to gain knowledge and confidence with her finances. The damaged parts began to thrive. Five years later—much to their surprise—Gloria

remarried her ex-husband. Neither one expected that outcome. But as they ended the dysfunctional money beliefs acquired over forty-two years, they found what was valuable in their lives—each other.

As many significant relationships as there are in this world, you'll discover just as many behaviors and routines with money. These behaviors and routines reveal a storehouse of money beliefs.

Reflect on a significant relationship in your life. How does money affect this relationship? Does one partner make all the decisions and retain all the power? Does one have all the knowledge? All the responsibility? Do you keep things separate or together? Why? Is there shame, blame, or secrecy between you? What is your story?

Write your musings in your journal. Pay attention to anything that pops into your mind. Remember, you're uncovering your unconscious beliefs about money. Even the smallest issue can lead you to a much bigger and more important belief. They all are important. Don't judge them; we want them in their pure, unadulterated form.

After you spend some time writing, glean the most important beliefs about money and relationships from your musings. Maybe you grew to believe that men are in charge of finances, or perhaps the opposite? Did you learn that whoever has the money has the power? What did you specifically learn?

 Record these in your Unexamined Beliefs section in the back of the book.

SPIRITUAL VIEWPOINT

Whether you consider yourself religious, spiritual, agnostic, or atheist, you absorb spiritual money messages from our culture. A perfect example is the classic message "money is the root of all evil." No matter what religion you are (or aren't), it is part of our culture and affects your life with money. To make matters worse, most of us are influenced by this bastardized version of the original message: "The love of money is the root of all evil." Not only has this spiritual money message influenced your life, but it isn't even the right one!

New spirituality imbeds lessons in its teachings as well as the ancient, organized religions of the world. In the last few years, you may have heard a lot about the book *The Secret*. This popular book gives us the secret to prosperity, health, relationships, and happiness. *The Secret* provides us with new beliefs about attracting abundance. But your other unexamined beliefs add their own spin to this new teaching. So, when you are unable to master *The Secret* overnight, these beliefs rear their ugly head, bringing with them unhealthy doses of blame and shame.

Terry was an old soul. Although still in his twenties, he was strong in his spiritual beliefs and his desire to make a difference in this world. When I asked him if he had any limiting beliefs with money he was quick to answer no—he knew God provided and that abundance was his. Yet as we spoke, he shared about being uncomfortable charging for his spiritual coaching—it wasn't the *right* thing to do. Consequently, his spiritual ministry was at a standstill because he found it difficult to support himself.

Spiritual beliefs often form around concepts of good and bad—right and wrong. They also revolve around faith and trust—desires and charity. You must examine your ethical beliefs as well as traditional or non-traditional religious and spiritual beliefs. Even if you lead a non-religious, secular life, your money beliefs are part of your everyday culture. So, in an effort not to leave any stone unturned, you must continue your search of spiritual money beliefs.

I n your journal, make a list of any spiritual money beliefs you discover. Remember, these may come in the form of ethical behaviors, doing right or wrong or being a righteous person. It may help to think of the Seven Deadly Sins: pride, envy, gluttony, lust, anger, covetousness, and sloth. How do beliefs associated with these seven sins relate to money?

(A while back, my sisters and I tried to remember these seven deadly sins, but none of us could recall them all. After some lively discussion, we looked them up and turned them into an anagram to commit them to memory—CPALEGS. Now, you can remember them too.)

List as many beliefs as you can, whether you think they are yours or not. Keep in mind that now is not the time for judgment. This list may include thriftiness as a virtue, generosity as spiritually moral or any number of things related to ethics, morals, and spirituality.

 When you are finished with the list, check off the ones that belong to you and record them in the Unexamined Beliefs section.

EDUCATIONAL ATTITUDE

School experiences generate powerful beliefs about how and why you operate in this world. In subtle ways you aren't aware of, they influence your relationships with money.

> I worked with Sally who insisted she was *bad* with money. Yet when she spoke of how she actually handled money, it was evident to me that she really was quite capable of making responsible decisions and, in fact, had been doing so her entire life. I questioned why she thought this way. After going round and round for a while, we discovered she thought she was bad with money because she was not good at math. School pounded that into her brain, and she mistakenly equated math with money! But the truth is math only quantifies financial decisions; it has nothing to do with making those decisions!

Education can indirectly influence our money beliefs. They affect not only your choice of college but also your experiences there.

> Dan, a twenty-five-year-old with a business degree, had a new career and was saddled with significant credit card debt that he accumulated during his college years. When we looked closely at how and why he had this debt, he mentioned that, although he had been accepted at an Ivy League school, his parents wanted him to attend the less expensive state university. He now realized that building credit card debt was his unconscious response to not being able to educate himself the way he wanted. One way or another, he had that expensive education!

As many people who believe an expensive education is important, there are just as many who believe being a *self-taught man* is even more important. These beliefs drive how they look at themselves and others to the same extent that beliefs about being an *educated man* do. Consequently, pride in being self-taught can keep you from acquiring new, important skills that could make you even more successful. One way or another, beliefs about the worth of education ultimately connect to money.

Take your journal and reflect on the importance of education in your family.

Did your parents encourage education?

Or did they see it as *optional?*

Was the type of school you went to important, or did it not matter?

Was it more important to get A's or to be socially accepted?

Make a list of educational beliefs that affected you and your money life. Choose those that seem most influential and write them in the Unexamined Beliefs section at the back of the book.

WORK VALUES

On the heels of education appear work beliefs. Often, they are tied together. The educational paths you choose lead you to your work life. Your money beliefs and what you find valuable control your choice of job and profession.

I did a workshop for twenty-something-year-olds just out of college who were starting new professional careers. During the limiting beliefs exercise, Caroline told me she didn't have any. She said her parents did a good job teaching her to be responsible with money. They told her the most important thing in life was to have a good, steady job with good benefits where she could stay for years. Later after more self-examination, she realized this could become a big limiting belief! She saw how her parents' belief might cause her to stay in a dead-end job with missed career opportunities and no personal fulfillment.

Your work choices are fraught with society's beliefs about what you should expect. We all *know* that individuals in certain helping professions—mental health and social workers—can't expect to make much money. We *know* that other helping professions—doctors and dentists—yield great financial success (and even may *believe* these individuals choose these careers only for the money). Teachers are seen as both underpaid and overpaid because of their extended summer breaks. For every profession, you can find a money belief that society has fed you. All of these beliefs influence your choice of career.

And once you have chosen that career, your money beliefs drive how you operate within that field.

At a recent workshop for private-practice, mental-health counselors, participants uncovered the limiting beliefs they possessed around fees for their services. Heather particularly felt it difficult to ask for full payment. Searching for limiting beliefs, she uncovered not only the general belief mentioned about her profession but also the belief that one shouldn't be paid for helping people. With this limiting belief, Heather would never be financially successful because she charged most of her time at low rates to help others instead of herself.

Money beliefs influence both your choices of career and your daily operation within your occupation. So it's important for you to find those beliefs; when you are financially conscious, you can see how those beliefs contribute to your overall fiscal well-being.

Write about your parents' work experiences. What do you remember most about how they modeled work?

Does your choice of work reflect your parents' experiences or anyone else's?

Did you accept their modeling or reject it?

How did your parents' work affect their finances?

How has your choice influenced your life?

List the work beliefs that shape your money life. Have you learned that financial success is more important than loving what you do, or that a helping profession results in empty pockets? What distinctive work beliefs drive your financial life? Choose the most prominent ones to list in your Unexamined Beliefs log.

A WORLD OF MONEY

The way you view the world influences your relationship with money. As Americans, we view having the biggest and the best as synonymous with *being* more. We look down our noses at other nations and their viewpoints without even gathering information to support our beliefs. We think we are the greatest and that everyone else wants to be in our shoes.

The economic mess we find ourselves in—along with the loss of world respect over the last decade—has started to crumble this belief. Who are we really? What does it really mean to be an American? What do we want to stand for?

One of my favorite quotes about America is from Alexis deTocqueville (1805-1859).

> I sought for the greatness and genius of America in her commodious harbors and her ample rivers—and it was not there ... in her fertile fields and boundless forests—and it was not there ... in her rich mines and her vast world commerce—and it was not there ... in her democratic Congress and her matchless Constitution—and it was not there. Not until I went into the churches of America and heard her pulpits flame with righteousness did I understand the secret of her genius and power. America is great because she is good, and if America ever ceases to be good, America will cease to be great.

To me, this is how Americans should evaluate themselves—by goodness, not financial resources. If we continue to make decisions based on money, we will cease to be great. It's time for us to examine the underlying beliefs that drive our American culture.

Y ou can begin to look at your worldview by investigating a few sources. Discussions of foreign policy are full of these beliefs; they fuel the current war. Political discussions in person, on the radio, or online yield good opportunities for investigating your worldviews about money. During political campaigns, the airwaves are full of messages—if you listen closely, you'll hear the money beliefs behind them.

What are some of the beliefs you are aware of right now or in the past? If you can't think of any easily, pick up a newspaper or read an online article.

 Write these down in your journal along with any other thoughts. Choose the most significant thoughts to record in your Unexamined Beliefs log.

Chapter III

IT'S MORE THAN YOU THINK!

ow you have an idea of what your unexamined money beliefs are and where they originated. Simply identifying them isn't enough though—you need to see how they affect your money. And while you look at how they influence your money, you'll discover how they shape other parts of your life. Beliefs are the underlying reason for the way you think, feel, and act. Money beliefs are your automatic responses to how you manage your money.

You usually aren't aware of your first response to these money beliefs. Often they entail feelings of some kind—either emotional or physical. Feelings of dread might envelop you, and sick feelings may erupt in your stomach. You may not even notice them anymore because they have been automatic for so long. But you should pay attention to these autonomic responses. With these alarms, your body alerts you that something is up—something you need to examine further.

Your next response may be a thought: "I shouldn't spend this money. How will I ever get ahead?" Or "oh no, the credit card bill just came in!" With these first thoughts come the underlying beliefs that influence how you deal with the situation at hand.

For example, "I shouldn't spend this money" may trigger a belief that your mother always thought you overspent. This goes further to "mother shouldn't control my life any longer." Then your response might be to spend anyway: "Screw it—I'm not a child anymore!"

"How will I ever get ahead" triggers hopelessness or the feeling you aren't even capable of dealing with finances. You feel it's not worth even trying because it won't work anyway. So you continue acting in ways that keep you firmly planted in those beliefs.

"Oh no, the credit card bill" reminds you of your irresponsibility—now and always. You ignore the bill or even throw it away, continuing patterns of irresponsibility that prove true once again; you are what you believe.

It's easy to see how these automatic responses keep you in dysfunctional money patterns. How else do money beliefs affect your life? Let's find out by looking at some important financial areas.

OVERALL ATTITUDE

Your overall attitude regarding money and finances is a good place to start your investigation. Is it fear? Obsession? Are you over responsible or under responsible? Do you feel stupid, maybe ashamed? Are you holier than thou or looking askance from your ivory tower? Do you always have plenty? Never enough? This overriding attitude is key to becoming financially conscious of your beliefs.

Some of us have an overwhelming fear of anything connected to money from growing up with too little (or even too much—like Mary mentioned before). Confronted with money decisions, you may be thrown into dark corners of despair. Because this fear takes you to places of doom and hopelessness, you avoid the topic or any interactions with money.

Jerry and Susan came into my office in this place of fear and impending doom. Jerry was seventy-four years old and still working—with no hope of retirement. He and his wife Susan already lived on all of his earnings, his social security, and his government pension—and there still wasn't enough to pay for a house with two mortgages in excess of fair market value. Susan was twenty years younger with health issues and she worried she would never have consistent earnings. They saw no hope for their financial situation—or their lives in general.

Fear had backed them into a corner with no hope for a solution. The stress caused Jerry to believe he would die working—never able to enjoy retirement. After examining their fear around finances, insolvency, and lack of future credit, they reluctantly began exploring the possibility of a short sale of their house. At first, because of unexamined beliefs, they couldn't see beyond the problems, but slowly the shame and blame lifted, and they began to see possible solutions.

Six months later, Jerry felt like a new man, enjoying retirement with an easier, part-time job. They rented a simple home in the place of their dreams, paid down other debt, and face life with hope and possibility.

Obsession with accumulating money is another overall attitude to explore. Television, movies, and tabloids flaunt the *good life* that money brings, so one easily falls prey to an attitude of spending more money at any cost. Working long hours at the expense of your relationships and families, you may soon lose sight of everything except more dollars and larger investment accounts.

The fable *King Midas* reminds us of what happens with the overwhelming quest for riches. King Midas received his wish for the touch of gold, but with all those riches, he was unable to drink or feed himself. He lost life itself! Obsession with money gives you gold-colored glasses through which you lose sight of all that is important.

Sometimes you unconsciously reject even having money. You don't want to be obsessed or driven with money so you lead *small* financial lives and end up with overall lives that are unnecessarily *small* and tight.

I know people who choose to live in tents or off the grid because they don't want money to *direct* their lives. I often wonder what opportunities or experiences they missed because of this. Isn't this obsession with having less ruling them just as powerfully as having more?

You may think that money is *dirty,* believing that those with money did something *evil* to get it—you *know* they will never do anything good with all their money. You may keep yourself in a small box of having just enough because *just enough* is for the *good* people of the world.

Sometimes ivory tower attitudes obstruct real relationships with those less fortunate. These attitudes don't make room for mistakes—for others or your-self; making perfect financial decisions is a constant vigil. When you do make mistakes (and we all do one time or another), you automatically fall into blame and shame because there is no room for free decision-making—you're afraid of becoming one of *them.* Relaxing around money is not an option!

The concept of *enough* is different for all of us because of our beliefs. Some of us always seem to have plenty and operate freely believing we will be taken care of.

> I always joked with my ex that whether he had $5 or $500 it always lasted a day. Having enough was never a worry of his!

Yet others believe there is never enough—in fact, the concept of enough may escape you. With constant worry about survival and yielding to the fickle fate of finance you are always on the edge of *almost* enough. Unfortunately, your concept of enough expands with any increase in income, and enough becomes the ever expanding *just enough.*

So you see how important it is to uncover your overall attitude about money. Are you fearful or relaxed with money matters? Does money have a healthy place in your life? Are you more comfortable with or without it? Just what is your overall attitude? Uncovering these issues is the key to driving your financial life!

H ave your journal close to you as you follow this visualization to help you access your overall attitude around money.

Close your eyes and take three deep breaths. Breathe in—and—out. In—and—out. In—and—out. Relax and let your imagination flow. Together, we're traveling on a journey. Imagine walking out the front door of your home. A path that wasn't there before stretches in front of you. It's gold and sparkly—kind of like the yellow brick road in the *Wizard of Oz*. You're not sure where it leads but begin following it.

You walk for a while feeling the cool, gentle breeze on your face. It's a glorious summer day, and the warmth of the sun is just right. Feeling the cool breeze and warm sun brings a smile to your face.

You look up and see a beautiful, spring-green, hot air balloon with sunbursts circling its sides floating lazily above you. You've always wanted to ride in a hot air balloon; you watch as it slowly descends and touches down right before you. The door of the basket opens, and you step in. Immediately, it begins to rise over the treetops into the beautiful, clear sky. The view is magnificent, and your vision is endless.

As you continue to rise, you see before you a beautiful patchwork of colors. You study it and realize it is the quilt of your current money life. Each patch in the quilt represents a different area that has influenced your life. You locate your earliest memory, your family of origin, your significant relationships, your education, your work, your spirituality, and your worldview. Each one provides a piece of the overall fabric of your money life. You find it fascinating how they all weave together—in and out, roundabout—all having a piece in the big picture.

As you see how they all come together, you are aware that there is an *overall feel* to the quilt enveloping all the separate pieces. You examine it further, taking as much time as you need to obtain a clear knowledge of this feeling. All of your monetary beliefs work together to form the essence of the quilt. Understanding the *feel* of the quilt will enable you to become financially conscious and economically aware.

When you're ready, answer these questions:

> What is the overall message or attitude that you see in your current financial life?
>
> What is the limiting belief that drives your overall attitude towards money?

 Record this limiting belief in the Unexamined Beliefs log.

You hear an eagle cry, and you turn toward the sound on the opposite side of the balloon. Surprised, you find a completely different view. The patches of the quilt shift, and you see the new vision for your financial quilt—the vision of where you are going. Once again the patches of the quilt represent those seven areas of your money life—your earliest memory, family of origin, significant relationships, education, work, spirituality, and world-view. Now they come together with a new message or attitude for you. Take time to understand the message fully.

When ready, answer this question:

What is the new vision and/or goal you want for your money life?

 Record this in Financial Visions section in the back of your book.

ABILITY AND RESPONSIBILITY

Now that you examined your overall attitude, let's look at some specific areas affected by your money beliefs. Feelings of ability and responsibility (or lack thereof) are important places to begin because you learn at an early age whether you can be *trusted* with finances.

> I've often wondered if I became an accountant because of my second-grade experience. Obviously, money was a big issue—important enough that there was a school-wide questionnaire. I know I was certainly uncomfortable not knowing the answer—after all, it stuck with me all these years. Maybe my belief of not being trustworthy or responsible enough led me to be an accountant where I could prove my worth and ability.

Sometimes being responsible at too early an age can impact you later in life.

> Charlie had a hard time finding a regular paying job that he enjoyed—he seemed to bounce from one job to another. Although he contributed regularly to the family finances, he was not the one providing a strong, financial foundation. When I asked Charlie and his wife about their childhood money memories, he talked of supporting himself since the age of ten. Family finances had been difficult as a child, and he knew he needed to help. At the age of ten, he became a door-to-door salesman for greeting cards and continued working odd jobs all through his childhood. During high school, he had a full-time job as well as attended school fulltime. Until our conversation, he hadn't been aware that his adult attitude toward work was a response to this over responsibility as a child.

Similarly, your relationship with money may reflect an overriding sense of irresponsibility in other parts of your life.

I know a young man who believes he can't do anything right and that he is a disappointment to everyone. Unfortunately, his behavior with money reinforces this belief. Although he has minor problems with money that could be handled easily, he reaffirms his irresponsibility by not dealing with a few unpaid bills. He keeps his phone's voicemail full because he doesn't want collection calls. And every time a friend, family member, or potential employer can't get in touch with him, he is reminded of just how irresponsible he is.

Or, you may have been in a relationship where you possessed no financial responsibility and now believe you are incapable of understanding.

Over twenty years ago, my mother was widowed. My father always handled the finances for the family, and even though we explained to Mom that Dad had provided well and she wouldn't have to worry about money, she had no concept of how much she had. The thought of buying a $20 sweater would throw her into a chaotic worry. Now, twenty years later, at ninety-one, her belief of incapability has become so strong that she is irrationally afraid of not having money.

Any beliefs of incapability and irresponsibility will grow stronger and stronger the longer they go unexamined. It's important to maintain a clear concept of just how capable and responsible you believe you are.

You will need your journal for this visualization exercise.

Close your eyes and take three deep breaths. Breathe in—and—out. Breathe in—and—out. Breathe in—and—out. Relax and let your imagination flow as we start another journey together.

Imagine walking out the front door of your home. Once again, you find that gold and sparkly path—the one like the yellow brick road in the *Wizard of Oz.* Not sure where you're going, you follow the path.

This time you find yourself walking along a country road. A pleasant fall day, you enjoy gazing at the trees with their beautiful shades of yellow, orange, and red. Occasionally, a chipmunk or rabbit scurries across the road in search of food. You smile as you see them so intent on their quest.

The road ends in the midst of five small cottages. You can't see anyone around, but the door to the first cottage is ajar, calling for you to enter. You open the door and find a table with a note next to $500. The note says, "This $500 is my gift to you. Please do with it what you want. The only thing you must do is tell me how you will spend it."

Decide how you would spend this money—no judgments allowed. Just go with your first thoughts. Write how you plan to use the $500 in your journal.

You leave this first cottage and open the door to the next. Like the first cottage, you discover a table and note, but this time you find $5,000. The note says, "This $5,000 is my gift to you. Please do with it what you want. The only thing I request of you is to tell me how you will spend it."

How will you spend the $5,000 differently than the $500? Think about this for a moment and then record it in your journal.

When you enter the third cottage, amazed, you see a note with $50,000 and the same request. Now you have more choices— what will you do?

With a little more thought, you write the list of how you will spend the $50,000 in your journal.

Hoping you are thinking along the correct lines, you open the door to the fourth cottage and astonishingly find $500,000. You have never seen this much money. The note clearly states it is all for you to do with as you want.

What will you do with all this money? Once again you comply, and as requested, you tell your unknown benefactor what you intend to do with the $500,000.

You find yourself unable to even imagine what you will find in that fifth cottage. As much as you try to tell yourself you are seeing things, you know that it really is $5,000,000. How could you possibly spend this much money? What will you do with these abundant resources?

Take your time to leave a note with details about all you intend to do with it.

As you close the door to that fifth and final cottage, you say a prayer of gratitude for all that money can buy. But you find all of this spending has stirred up some feelings and beliefs about what you *should* do with the money and how you *should* spend it.

How did you feel making these spending decisions?

Was it easy? Or did it get difficult at some point? If so, which point?

How did it feel having responsibility for these spending decisions?

Are you anxious? Confused? Afraid? Free? Anything else?

What limiting beliefs surfaced regarding your ability and responsibility? Do you feel capable making these decisions? Was it easy to be responsible for this money? How do you feel about making money decisions? Write these beliefs in your Unexamined Beliefs log.

Now, how would you *like* to feel about handling this money? Record your vision for your ability and responsibility in your Financial Visions log.

SPENDING AND SPENDING PLANS

Obviously, your beliefs affect how you spend your money. Do you spend too much—or not enough? Do you deprive yourself of little needs and wants only to splurge on big-ticket items? Do you *comfort spend* to make yourself feel better? Are you living back in the Great Depression? Do you drive yourself crazy with too much structure and no flexibility? Or do you panic at the thought of budgets or restrictions? The answers to these questions reflect the money beliefs underlying them.

During challenging economic times, we hear about the results of spending beyond our means. Sub-prime mortgages and unsecured credit card debt are just two of the problems that sent our economy into a recession. It is our money beliefs, fueled by society's beliefs and values that lured us into these traps. These beliefs, amplified by family beliefs, make it easy to fall prey to overspending (and sometimes under spending).

During good economic times, the media and advertising plant the notion that our wealth and the world's wealth are bottomless and that our possessions measure our value. Our homes get bigger and our *things* grow. Our incomes rise and with each increase, so does our spending. With the credit brakes screeching, we stumble over the edge unable to see out of the abyss.

How did we get to this point? Sometimes, it's because you grew up in a family where money was scarce and crisis was plentiful. The notion of a financially free life may be too far out of your comfort zone. You relied on saying, "I can't really afford that" or "times are tough now." The thought of having enough and becoming one of *them* is too much. So, you continually make bad financial decisions to keep yourself in the overspending box where you are comfortable.

You continue to dream of being one of those *other* people who know how to stick to a budget. And you find plenty of advice from friends and family about how to do it.

Bill told me he received advice years ago that was so easy; if people just followed it, they would have immediate financial success. The advice? "Live on half of what you earn and invest the rest." Sounds simple enough—right? Not to those of us brought up in families that spent not only today's paycheck but also next week's, next month's, and next year's!

Following this advice is impossible because our spending beliefs keep us in such small financial boxes that we don't know where to begin. Just hearing this advice starts our stomachs churning. We lower our heads in shame, and blame ourselves for being so stupid. And the stupider we feel, the more we spend to comfort ourselves.

On the other hand, if you were *lucky* to be part of a budgeting family, you think you have it all under control: "I never spend anything without planning for it." For you, there is no such thing as an impulse buy. You learned there's no room for buying anything *frivolous*. Unfortunately, no one ever defined frivolous.

Joan lived an austere life buying only life's essentials. With no fluff in her spending, she couldn't understand why she faced financial difficulties. When we did a spending exercise, no matter how much money she visualized spending, she never included anything special for herself. Yet, in real life, she had substantial credit card debt. As we delved into these extra expenses, she discovered her credit card debt was from larger, extravagant things she had bought after being frustrated by never buying anything special for herself. Her austere budget constantly backed her into a corner until she broke out in a spending spree.

Comfort spending is also a common pattern. Instead of facing uncomfortable emotions or situations, you may run away and reach for your favorite addiction—food, tobacco, alcohol, or whatever else. For some of us, that *whatever* is spending.

Eileen had a close friend who recently died. Her friend's husband was shocked to discover boxes and bags of new, unworn clothes that his wife purchased during her battle with cancer. She spent thousands and thousands of dollars running away from the reality of her impending death.

Spending on others at your own expense may be a reaction to learned family patterns. Over (or under) generosity may be at the root of your spending patterns.

At a recent workshop, Lynn discovered that her family's belief in sharing affected her finances. Growing up she said one wouldn't dare say, "Can I have a Coke?" No, instead, you would say, "Would you like to share a Coke with me?" Even if it was just a sip, the other person would comply. Now, as an adult, her finances were at risk because of always buying something special for her family and friends—she was sharing herself into the poor farm!

Having too much financial support from your family can result in dysfunctional spending habits.

Jill was from a wealthy family that always provided well for her. Now in her forties, she has no concept of how to handle her own finances. Her parents always bailed her out of difficult financial situations, and she has no idea how to support herself or how much money she needs. She spends indiscriminately and finds herself constantly confused. Worse than that, she describes herself as a spoiled brat! With a belief like that, it's hard to move forward responsibly.

Obsessing over frugality may be your spending pattern. So caught up with not spending, you are unable to enjoy the simple joys of life.

My son Kilian helped his father clean out his deceased grandparents' home. He knew Grammy was a spendthrift who never wasted a thing so he wasn't surprised to find old margarine containers and plastic bags. But Kilian was greatly saddened to find a ream of copy paper that his father had given Grammy years before to use for writing letters to her many friends (stationery would have been too extravagant). Although it cost less than five dollars, Grammy never allowed herself this one simple pleasure; instead, she continued to write on the back of any used paper she found.

Our approach to spending gives us another view of how beliefs affect our overall financial life. Is spending just something that happens? Or do you maintain a clear plan of what your intentions are and where you want to go? Are you conscious of how you make your financial decisions? Some of us maintain an organized approach to spending—we would never consider working without a budget. Others break out in hives just thinking of *budgeting*. (This is why I usually refer to a budget as a spending plan.)

Without a financial plan or vision to move forward—combined with a spending plan to lead you there—you are doomed to repeat these dysfunctional patterns. Only by taking the time to work with the underlying beliefs can you begin to function with financial integrity.

Spending patterns have many faces, and everyone has their own spending beliefs. By working with what is underneath the spending, you can uncover unhealthy money beliefs that drive your spending decisions.

Y ou will need your journal again for this visualization exercise.

Close your eyes and take three deep breaths. Breathe in—and—out. In—and—out. In—and—out. Relax and let your imagination flow. Imagine strolling out the front door of your home to that now familiar gold and sparkly path. Unsure of where it leads, you eagerly follow it.

The path takes you beside a meandering river. Lush, green grass thrives along the riverbanks, and you take your shoes off to experience the cool blades of grass tickling your toes as you walk.

You encounter a fork in the river and find a red kayak. You climb into the kayak and begin paddling. You're amazed at how easy it is to maneuver and how safe you feel being this close to the water. When you feel comfortable, you decide where to paddle. To the right, you see a sign—Planned Spending. To the left, it says Unplanned Spending. You choose to paddle to the right—to Planned Spending.

You glide into the Planned Spending Pond. You look around and take in the scenery. What does it look like? What color is it? Are there any sounds? What do you smell?

In your journal, describe the Planned Spending Pond and answer these questions. What do you find? How does it feel? Is it comfortable being here? Close your eyes and take another deep breath. Is there a message for you in the Planned Spending Pond? Record that message.

You decide to investigate the other pond, paddle back to the fork, and turn down to the Unplanned Spending Pond. Once again, you glance around the pond. What does it look like? What color is the pond? What sounds do you hear? What do you smell?

Take your journal and describe the Unplanned Spending Pond. Answer these questions. What do you find? How does it feel? Is it comfortable being here? What message does Unplanned Spending have for you?

Once you are finished writing, you continue to paddle back and forth—between the Planned Spending Pond and Unplanned Spending Pond. Soon you discover that unlike you believed originally, there's not a fork in the river—but actually a stream connecting the two ponds in a large circle. It's an odd discovery, and you wonder what it means.

Take your time coming back by taking three deep breaths. Breathe in—and out. Breathe in—and out. Breathe in—and out.

Contemplate what you have written in your journal about both Spending Ponds.

What do these two ponds mean to you? Where are you comfortable?

Is there a pattern to your spending? What limiting beliefs surfaced?

 Is there a message for you in this exercise? Write these in your Unexamined Beliefs log.

What is your vision for your future with spending?

 Write this down in your Financial Visions log.

ACCESS TO CREDIT, DOORWAY TO DEBT

Spending and debt can go hand in hand, especially when you spend in excess of your earnings. Not surprisingly, this debt occurs as a direct consequence of your beliefs. Are you comfortable with debt? Do you take it too seriously—or not seriously enough? Does any amount of debt fill you with fear? Does too much debt push you into hopelessness? Answers to these questions can help you uncover your underlying debt beliefs and lead you down the road to financial awareness.

Some people are afraid of debt and let fear drive their decisions.

Twenty-two years ago, my business partner Janet and I purchased our office condominium. I shared information with my father about the real estate investment and the size of the mortgage we incurred. His reaction? He wished he had been as courageous as we were. He had always wanted (and needed) a new building for his car dealership, but his fear of new debt stopped him in his tracks. Now, years later, he regretted the decision that kept him in a too-small facility hampering the growth and efficiency of his business.

When fear of debt stops you from living a full life or turns you away from meaningful opportunities, you need to examine the beliefs behind it. Are these beliefs working for you—or against you? Is someone else's fear taking away your freedom of choice? Sometimes, too much debt isn't the problem.

More often than not, though, too much debt *is* the problem—a big problem.

Approximately 640 million credit cards circulate in the United States with about 750 to 800 billion dollars in balances (based upon Federal Reserve figures). The average American has four credit cards with access to $19,000 in credit. About 60 percent carry credit card

> balances instead of paying in full each month, and that isn't the worst of it. Credit card companies made over 43 billion dollars in over-limit, late payment, and balance transfer fees in 2004. (I can only imagine how much they made in 2009!)

Clearly, credit card debt hugely impacts your life. Our society runs on credit cards—a TV ad even shows the world stopping when a person uses cash. For some transactions like renting a car, you can't use cash—you must have a card.

It's been drilled into us that we must maintain a great credit history to get ahead in this world. "The FICO® score has become the single most important indicator used by lenders to predict whether you will repay (a loan)," according to the New York Times. Our society revolves around FICO scores and the credit world; financial guru Suze Orman even sells a FICO Kit. And your insurance premiums can be increased or decreased based on your FICO score.

But, I believe you are more than your FICO score—and I hope you do too. Just knowing, obsessing, or cleaning up your FICO score is not enough—you need to uncover and understand the beliefs behind that debt reported on your FICO score.

As a child, you probably learned that credit cards are a part of everyday life. When you came of age (eighteen according to credit card companies), credit cards waited for you with open arms. Young adults not only have average credit card debt of $4,088 but also average student loan debt of $20,000. They spend 24 percent of their income on debt payments!

Society paves the way for dysfunctional lives with debt. Before twenty-somethings know what hit them, they are drowning in debt without the tools to cope. And because of the role credit and debt play in our society, young adults believe that credit and debt are *rights*. It takes years to learn the hard lesson that credit and debt are not rights but rather *privileges* that come with responsibilities. By then, it is often too late—the confusion between rights and privileges leaves them with the second highest rate of personal bankruptcy in the nation.

Because you likely had such a poor start with debt, it continues to plague you throughout your life. And because of ready access to more credit, the saga continues with quick fixes to your debt problems. New credit cards and balance transfer offers arrive every day luring you into newer and *better* credit cards. Rarely, if ever, do credit card companies ask you to close the old credit cards—in fact, you discovered that doing so would hurt your FICO score! Instead, you are handed the *opportunity* to expand your debt one more time.

Too much debt keeps you in dysfunctional spending patterns. Credit card debt puts you in tight financial boxes that prevent you from freedom in spending decisions. Pushed into the corner of your box, you try to spend your way out. The new spending only makes your box tighter, pushing you further and further into the corners of despair.

Just this weekend, I spoke to my oldest son about the financial freedom that comes when we aren't bogged down with excessive debt. I have met too many clients over too many years who were not able to take advantage of new careers or investment opportunities because debt kept them from freedom of choice. The *right* to credit narrows future choices.

To be free to live the full life you deserve, it is crucial to examine your beliefs around debt and credit.

You will need your journal for this exercise.

Close your eyes and take three deep breaths. Breathe in—and—out. In—and—out. In—and—out. Relax and let your imagination flow. Let's start on another journey!

The gold and sparkly path extends right outside your door again. You gladly step on it ready for another adventure.

The path winds through a lush, green meadow. Beautiful wild-flowers—black-eyed Susans, tiger lilies, and daisies—line the sides of the path and sway in the warm breeze as you walk. The tall grass swishes softly as the wind blows through it.

Eventually, you stumble upon a building—kind of square and non-descript. Something about it intrigues you. Beautiful sea roses surround the entire building, and their smell relaxes you. You approach the door where a large welcome sign says "Come in, we've been waiting for you."

You open the door and find yourself in the room of *past debt*.

> What does the room look like? What colors, sounds, and smells does it have?
>
> How do you feel in it?
>
> What is it saying to you? Does it have a message for you?

Describe the room of *past debt* in your journal. Is there a general feeling to the room? What colors, sounds, and smells does it have? Write down the room's message for you.

When you finish, you notice a door in the back wall. You open the door and find yourself in the room of *present debt*.

> What does this room look like? What colors, sounds, and smells does it have?
>
> How do you feel in it?
>
> What is it saying to you? Does it have a message for you?

Describe the room of *present debt* in your journal. Record the message the room has for you.

When you are finished, you notice yet another door in the back wall. You open the door and find yourself in the room of *future debt*.

What does this final room look like? What colors, sounds, and smells does it have?

How do you feel in it?

What is it saying to you? Does it have a message for you?

Describe the room of *future debt* in your journal. Write its message for you. Did your experiences in the rooms of *past* and *future debt* change how you feel about the room of *present debt*?

You leave the room and find yourself back on the path in the lush green meadow. You enjoy the beautiful flowers on your journey. Take your time coming back by taking three deep breaths. Breathe in—and—out. In—and—out. In—and—out.

 When you're back, write the limiting debt belief(s) that you uncovered in your Unexamined Beliefs log.

What new vision do you have for your life with debt as a result of this exercise? Changing your vision can be difficult, but it is possible!

 Record your vision in the Financial Visions section.

RELATIONSHIPS

Whether you know it or not, money beliefs affect all of your relationships—not only the relationships with your spouses or your children but with everyone you encounter in a given day. The reality is, finances can run and ruin your relationships.

Your beliefs influence your relationships with people on the street. Pay attention to what goes through your mind when you see a homeless person begging for change. How does this message affect how you relate to them? Or how do you treat the Wal-Mart greeter or the checkout person? These encounters provide you with clues about how money impacts your relationships.

As you might expect, beliefs shape your relationships with friends and relatives. You may have been taught that any interaction between money and friends or relatives is doomed to failure—but is it? If you are clear about your beliefs and expectations before heading into financial interactions, it doesn't have to be doomed. Unspoken beliefs get us into trouble, rearing their ugly heads and placing the relationship at risk.

Recently, I loaned money to a relative. We were clear up front about the repayment arrangement. The time for repayment came, and there was no payment or communication. Immediately, my inner dialogue started with those learned money beliefs: "I never should have loaned money to a relative. I was stupid to have thought they would pay. Now, we'll never be able to have a good relationship again. The family has been ruined!"

Instead of listening to those voices, I stopped. What did I really believe? What did I want for this relationship? What was my responsibility in this? I decided to communicate instead of listening to those beliefs and falling into despair. After our discussion, although the loan wasn't paid in full, I now knew the facts. Together we came to a new agreement that worked for both of us. More importantly, I was able to prove that those *learned* money beliefs weren't my truth—I wasn't stupid, and it was still the right thing to do. The family wasn't ruined; in fact, it felt stronger than ever and open communication was now the norm.

Money influences the relationships with your children in ways you never intended. Parents can easily use money as a tool for maintaining control. You can be *stingy* with your money to prevent your children from doing things you don't want them to do, or you can be overly generous and unconsciously keep them dependent on you. And, sometimes your own financial actions and irresponsibility can keep your children feeling insecure all their lives.

It has been interesting watching my three sons develop their individual styles with money. They all grew up in the same family; yet they have very different attitudes. John, the oldest (remember his credit card lesson at six), not surprisingly, started his career selling and providing customer service for a major credit card company. He likes to spend and has a knack for manipulating his finances to find ways to make sure he has enough to buy what he wants. My middle son Kilian doesn't need money to survive—he's happy on just what he has now—like his father. And my youngest, Evan, is a wheeler/dealer. He always finds a way to sell something to be able to get what he wants. With each of them, I can easily find a parental belief that contributed to their lives with money!

It's important to be aware of how your beliefs impact your children. They need to discover the money beliefs that work for them—not you. It can be difficult to see adult children handling their finances differently than you would.

It's important to offer guidance and advice in a way that allows them to make their own choices—and yes—sometimes their own mistakes.

Obviously, your money beliefs influence the significant others in your life. With two people—each with his/her own beliefs—it forms a natural arena for conflict. Money management can easily become a power play. Who makes the decisions? Who has access to the money? Are responsibilities shared, or does one person have all the burdens—as well as the control?

> Because I'm an accountant and finances are my game, it seemed natural that I would handle the money for our family, and my husband was happy to turn over the reins. But over the years, I slowly built up resentment for having to do all the work. He slowly started not to care. He was never asked for an opinion so he just didn't get involved.
>
> Eventually, we recognized the dysfunction in this arrangement and came up with a new routine—a new routine that surfaced dysfunctional beliefs. Yes, I had all the responsibility, but that meant I kept all the power and control. With both of us involved, we leveled the playing field and faced not only money issues but also those other, more difficult issues. My excuse of being the *expert* masked my need for control—and his lack of involvement yielded him plenty of opportunity for blame.

If you take time to examine dysfunction in your relationships, you can usually find a link to finances. Check it out sometime, and you'll be surprised where those money beliefs lurk!

Y ou will need your journal for this exercise.

Close your eyes and take three deep breaths. Breathe in—and—out. In—and—out. In—and—out. Relax and let your imagination flow.

You saunter out your door onto the gold and sparkly path. Much to your surprise, the path loops around to the back door of your home. As you enter the house, you find yourself floating above the room and above your own body.

As the unemotional, unbiased observer, you study your own interaction with your significant other (or perhaps a close friend or family member). You hover above as an unattached counselor brought in to *fine tune* the relationship. As the observer, you watch as you conduct a conversation with the other person regarding money. You have worked with these individuals for some time and have learned the patterns of how they operate in all areas of their life—but most importantly around money. You continue to watch for a while and observe many interesting things.

When you are finished, you go into the next room, sit at your desk, and begin working on the final report, documenting what you have found. Write about these people that you have been counseling. How do they interact with each other around money? What is important about the intangible side of their money life? The following questions might help you in compiling your report:

Who makes the decisions about spending?

Does anyone do secret spending?

Is there blame or shame around the other's money habits?

Who controls the money? Who has the power with money?

Is money used to manage the other person?

Does either person avoid financial responsibilities? Are money issues ignored?

If there are children, how do money issues affect them?

What limiting beliefs drive the individuals' shared financial life?

 Write these discoveries in your Unexamined Beliefs log.

 The last section of the report is your vision for these people. What needs to change to strengthen the couple? What do you envision for their future financial life? Write this vision in your Financial Visions log.

WORK

Financial beliefs also affect your work life. The value you attach to your job often is more about the money than the intangibles that enhance or detract from your overall life. The term *golden handcuffs* comes from knowing that the lure of pay and perks keeps an executive chained to a job during times of change. These arrangements hope to keep you from thinking too hard about making any career moves.

Acceptance or rejection of certain jobs and professions relates to your beliefs.

> I met a young man at the golf course management school my son attends. Jared told me how difficult it had been for his parents to accept him going to this school. Both college professors, the thought of him attending a trade school rather than a four-year college was hard to reconcile with their beliefs about what his career path should be.

Although certainly these beliefs also revolve around education and *worthy* professions, you can find the connection back to money beliefs.

Your beliefs drive how you operate within your chosen profession.

> Beth, a counselor I worked with, lamented that she had a hard time asking for her full fee when she knew her client was struggling, not only with finances, but also with other life challenges. How could she add to his/her angst by asking for full payment? Wasn't she as a counselor supposed to help people?

You may find it easy to locate money beliefs behind your work-related decisions and behaviors. Great—you are becoming more financially conscious!

Kristy, longing to have her own business, would start her own consulting business and then constantly worry about money. Her fear of failure would cause her to bounce back and forth between her own business and a salaried position in the corporate world. An examination of her family beliefs uncovered an entrepreneurial father who always had financial difficulties. She grew up hearing him complain and fight with his wife about money. His fears and stresses as an entrepreneur unwittingly became hers.

When you think of how your job or career represents happiness in your life, it's important to disconnect the dollar from the job. Without doing so, you easily continue in an unfulfilling and personally draining job. What's more, the stresses from staying in those places for too long can create many more far-reaching problems.

Have your journal ready for this exercise.

Close your eyes and take three deep breaths. Breathe in—and—out. In—and—out. In—and—out. Relax and let your imagination flow.

The gold and sparkly path appears at your front door. By this time, you know you are on your way to an adventure; you continue merrily along—not truly paying attention to the path. In your own little world enjoying the day, the path abruptly ends.

You discover yourself in front of your workplace, immediately evoking certain emotions. Surprised, you take a few moments to understand your reaction fully. What is the feeling—where does it come from? Is this feeling with you every day that you are at work?

You enter through the door where your boss and co-workers meet you. Perhaps, a client also greets you. With each person, identify your emotional response; take a few moments to analyze the response. What emotions do you feel? What causes the response?

You observe your place of work—not in the usual way when you are busy working—but as someone trying to gather the feelings, beliefs, and values of the workplace. For example, is the bottom line the most important aspect? Analyze the atmosphere of the office. Is it cozy and relaxed? Does it feel more like a big family? Or perhaps you feel on edge waiting for the axe to fall. As you pick up those *workplace* feelings, beliefs, and values, see how they coordinate with your own *personal* feelings, beliefs, and values.

After a time, you say your farewell and leave. You follow the path back to your home, your heart, and your body. You take three deep breaths: breathe in—and out, in—and out, in—and out.

In your journal, answer these questions:

> What does it feel like? Is it cold and unwelcoming—or warm and comforting?

> What are its overriding beliefs and values? Do you feel suffocated or buoyed by them?

> How do you feel here? Are you excited, nervous, secure, or perhaps depressed?

How do your beliefs and values relate to this place?

How do these relate to money and finance?

How do your money beliefs fit here?

Review your answers and write down any other important observations you found. Describe your place of work in these intangible ways.

 When finished, think about what you wrote and record any limiting beliefs in your Unexamined Beliefs log.

Now, close your eyes again and imagine this place—or another place of work—in a new space. In this new space, your personal beliefs and values and the values of your work are in complete agreement—one supports the other.

What does this new space look like? How does it relate to your current work environment?

What is your vision for work?

 Write it in your Financial Visions log.

ABUNDANCE

The spiritual movement yielded new meaning for abundance and money. Where once financial abundance was only about accumulating more money, it has grown to include concepts like the law of attraction, universal abundance, and money as a form of energy. A Google search of *financial abundance* brings up website after website. Here are just a few I found:

Seven Steps to Financial Abundance

Attracting Financial Abundance

Financial Abundance – Thriving Now

The Financial Abundance Factor

Spiritual Road to Financial Abundance

Create Unlimited Financial Abundance

and even

The Dark Side of Financial Abundance

Tips on how to attain financial abundance is everywhere including views on how you can, or cannot, manifest abundance in your life. Although I believe in the concept, its presentation, along with old learned responses, can unfortunately stir up blame and shame: "If I only was a better person," or "If only I had more faith," or "I guess I'm just not getting it" leaves one confused and discouraged.

A personal understanding of *abundance* must accompany an examination of what *lack, enough,* and *deserving* mean to you. Without an in-depth look at these concepts, you can't find your own beliefs around abundance.

Everyone interprets these terms differently. What is abundant for one may be scarcity for another. Enough for some means *barely enough;* for others, it means *more than enough.* Some believe they're entitled or *deserve* it, while others think it must be *earned.* It is important to take time to see how abundance plays out in your life. Are you comfortable with it? Or is the concept too far out there?

Years ago, I joined a women's weekly counseling group. Every week we met to support each other with various issues. A facilitator helped us delve into areas with which we all struggled. I remember Dawn wrestling each week with abundance. She understood the law of attraction, asking for what she wanted, acting and feeling like she already had it, and all the other abundance concepts. She was an expert at *letting go and letting God.* Yet, week after week, we heard her complain about nothing happening—about not being able to afford anything—about her life being on hold or stagnant.

In the quest for abundance exists that difficult place between action and inaction. When do your *actions* control the situation and when do your *inactions* control it? When do you push too hard and when do you not push hard enough? These are difficult questions, but your beliefs around lack, deserving, enough, and abundance will help you find the answers.

Close your eyes and take three deep breaths as we depart on a journey to the ocean of unlimited financial resources. Breathe in—and—out. In—and—out. In—and—out. Relax and let your imagination flow. Imagine walking out the front door of your home onto the gold and sparkly path.

The path winds along a river flowing at a slow, lazy pace. Through the beautiful blue water, you see all the way to the bottom where fish glide over a bed of multi-colored rocks. Every now and then, a fish jumps through the surface and falls back down in a waterfall of rainbow-colored droplets.

Eventually, the river widens, and its waters flow faster and faster.

The fish jump even more playfully as they near an opening into a huge body of water—an ocean. You locate no shoreline in any direction; this ocean seems to have endless bounds. In the Ocean of Unlimited Financial Resources, the water is even more beautiful and sparkly than the river. You can no longer see the multi-colored rocks in the bottom as it also seems to have endless depth. The Ocean of Unlimited Financial Resources has no beginning and no end.

As you gaze over this magnificent body of water, a dolphin playfully rises to the surface and invites you to join it, "Come, come with me." With no hesitation, you dive in and follow the dolphin. The dolphin leads you to a number of ocean caves.

The first cave it guides you to is the cave of *lack*. You swim in and look around. What does it look like? What do you find there? What colors, sounds, and smells do you notice? What emotions do you feel? How do you feel in the cave of lack?

In your journal, write or draw your impressions of the cave of *lack*. Before you leave this cave, take a deep breath—in and out—is there a message for you in the cave of *lack*? Write it in your journal.

You leave this cave and follow the dolphin into the second cave, the cave of *deserving*. You swim in and peer around. What does it look like? What do you find there? What colors, sounds, and smells do you notice? What emotions does it evoke?

How do you feel in the cave of *deserving*?

Write your impressions of the cave of *deserving* or draw a picture.

Before you leave, take a deep breath—in and out—is there a message for you in the cave of *deserving*? Write it in your journal.

You follow the dolphin out of the cave of *deserving* and into the cave of *enough*. You swim in and look around. What does it look like? What do you find there? What colors, sounds, and smells do you find?

How do you feel in the cave of *enough*?

Write what you see and feel in the cave of *enough*. Draw a picture if you like. Once again, before you leave, take a deep breath—in and out—is there a message for you in the cave of *enough*?

At last, you get to the cave of *abundance,* which you'd seen in the distance. The dolphin leads you into the cave and shows you around. What does it look like? What do you find there? What colors, sounds, and smells surround you?

How do you feel in the cave of *abundance*?

Write what you find in the cave of *abundance*—or draw a picture. Still in the cave of abundance, you swim around and enjoy its gifts—all it has to offer. After some time, the dolphin leads you to another entrance through which you swim. Somehow not surprised, you find yourself in your heart, in your body, and in your home.

Before she leaves, the dolphin has a final message for you— what is it? What does she want you to know? Write this in your journal.

Take three deep breaths before you return. Breathe in—and—out.
In—and—out. In—and—out.

Read what you have written in your journal. What limiting beliefs
did you illuminate during your time with the dolphin?

 Write these in your Unexamined Beliefs log.

What new vision do you have for your life with abundance?

 Record these in the Financial Visions section.

Chapter IV

DO THIS, NOT THAT

You have now uncovered money beliefs in seven areas of your life—your earliest memory, family of origin, significant relationships, education, work, spirituality, and worldview. You've also discovered how these beliefs affect seven facets of your life. Congratulations, you've taking significant steps on your way to becoming financially conscious! But now what? What do you do with these unexamined money beliefs?

You follow three simple steps:

1. State it.

2. Debate it.

3. Recreate it.

These three simple steps will lead you to the fulfillment of your financial goals and visions. As a Certified Empowerment Trainer, one of the basic concepts of the Empowerment Institute was the *Shift from Pathology to Vision*—a shift from focusing on what doesn't work in your life to what you actually want. In this current economic world, it's easy to see how focusing on financial gloom and doom traps us in a place of paralysis and powerlessness. It keeps us focusing on problems instead of creatively moving toward solutions.

What do I mean? The Empowerment Institute describes the process as the planting of a garden. When you start a garden from scratch, you focus on the flowers or vegetables in full bloom not the removal of rocks, roots, and weeds. You concentrate on the seeds and not the weeds: the outcomes not the obstacles. Weeds involve tedious removal, but cultivating flowers is motivating. Envisioning the blossoming garden keeps you motivated through the work of readying the garden space. In the words of the Institute, "We are motivated to grow by the power of our dreams rather than our problems."

Similarly, you can solve your financial problems by focusing on your financial goals and visions rather than today's problems. To shift from today's problems to that vision, you need clear, examined beliefs, providing you the foundation and motivation to make change happen.

STEP ONE: STATE IT

To begin you need to state your uncovered beliefs as clearly and concisely as possible. *State It* gets to the root issues by restating your beliefs in plain, simple language. Because it was your first glimpse at a belief, the language you first used to record that belief in your journal may be imprecise; but it was important to record your initial thoughts about the belief.

Now you need to clarify what the belief really means. You need to state it in clear, crisp language. You need to define the beliefs as purely and succinctly as possible.

> In my first memory of money (the second-grade questionnaire), I simply knew I was in the dark. I should have known the answer to that financial question, but my parents didn't tell me. Either I was stupid or couldn't be trusted—or both. My initial unexamined belief would have been *my parents think I'm stupid and don't trust me with financial information.*
>
> Over the years, that initial belief morphed and strengthened into more than that. That strengthened belief must be restated as clearly as possible. So the restatement of my belief becomes *I can't be trusted knowing about money.*

Here are some other examples of restated beliefs from the stories and examples in this book below:

1. I can't be trusted knowing about money.

2. I can avoid paying for things by manipulating money.

3. Without money, I am nothing.

4. Good people don't have money (or money is dirty).

5. I am bad (or irresponsible) with money.

6. I need an expensive education to be successful.

7. I need a steady, reliable job at all costs.

8. I shouldn't be paid for helping people.

9. There's no such thing as too much money.

10. I will never have enough money for what I need.

11. Budgets don't work, especially for me.

12 Spending money on myself is frivolous.

13. He who dies with the most toys wins.

14. Debt scares me.

15. I should never loan money to a relative.

16. I can control my children with money.

17. Only I can handle the family's money correctly.

18. I make too much money to change jobs.

19. Independent women handle their own money alone.

20. The world is abundant for everyone but me.

Notice the simple statements of big limiting beliefs. Stated as facts using few words, they pack powerful meanings. It may feel strange to restate them in this way because you don't really want to believe them. But don't worry about that—we'll deal with that in Step 2. For now, just state the limiting belief in its own stark reality.

Are the beliefs you recorded in the Unexamined Beliefs log stated in clear language?

Spend time discovering each statement's core belief. Remember it's important to get to the heart of the belief. Have you found the belief underneath the belief? Write and rewrite the belief until you understand it without a doubt.

 Record these clear, concise beliefs in the Restated Beliefs log in the back of your book.

STEP TWO: DEBATE IT

Next, you'll debate whether or not those beliefs are true for you—not for anyone else—just for you. You will prove or disprove these beliefs in your life.

> My friend Donna has a wonderful way of describing how to look at things a little differently. When stuck in black-and-white thinking, she'll ask, "Can you turn the box a little?" In other words, if we always look at something from the same viewpoint, we'll always see things the same way.

Now let's shift the box, change your viewpoint, and perhaps find something new. What if this belief isn't true? Can you find evidence to support a new way of thinking?

> I worked with Sally who *knew* she couldn't take care of herself. She talked of always needing to rely on others. I pointed out she was 45 and still alive and suggested that maybe she had taken care of herself by finding the right people in her life, like her loving husband. By turning the box, she could say she was capable and could believe that one truth. She also agreed that she was excellent at quantifying their financial issues and was a whiz at spreadsheets. Wasn't this a step in taking care of herself? That was truth number two. Knowing they were in financial straits, she called me to help solve the problem. There was truth number three. She was capable of taking care of herself!

Debate It involves finding facts that will support a new belief. It doesn't have to be three truths as in the example above; you may find just one strong truth disproving the old belief, or you may find a long list of reasons. The important thing is to find facts that support what you really want to believe—what your own personal truths are. Remember no one but you can find the facts to prove or disprove a particular money belief.

Working with some of the restated beliefs from above, here are some disproving facts:

1. I can't be trusted knowing about money.

   a. I know a lot about money from the things I read.

   b. I am trustworthy because people trust me with other things.

2. I can avoid paying for things by manipulating money.

   a. I end up paying more because of interest and penalties.

   b. Credit card companies use me to make money.

   c. I still have to pay.

3. Without money, I am nothing.

   a. I love the outdoors, and it costs nothing.

   b. With or without money, at my deepest core I am the same person.

4. Good people don't have money (or money is dirty).

   a. Oprah Winfrey

   b. Jimmy Carter

   c. Warren Buffett

5. I am bad (or irresponsible) with money.

   a. I always look for bargains.

   b. I've made it this far so I must be doing something right.

   c. I'm good with money compared to others.

6. I need an expensive education to be successful.

    a. Bill Gates didn't graduate from college.

    b. Peter Jennings

    c. Lance Armstrong

7. I need a steady, reliable job at all costs.

    a. I hate what I do.

    b. My health is more important than my job.

    c. I want to experience new opportunities.

8. I shouldn't be paid for helping people.

    a. Dr. Phil

    b. I need to support myself to be able to help others.

9. There's no such thing as having too much money.

    a. King Midas

    b. Imelda Marcos & her shoes

    c. My relationships are more important than having more money.

10. I will never have enough money for what I need.

    a. I survived this far so it must have been enough.

    b. Compared to others, I have more than enough.

11. Budgets don't work.

    a. I'm always confused about what I have because I don't have a plan.

    b. I make the choices in my spending plan.

    c. Putting my plan on paper helps me make clear, well thought-out choices.

12. Spending money on myself is frivolous.

    a. I take life seriously; my needs/wants are not frivolous.

    b. I need to spend money to live and flourish.

    c. I am important.

13. He who dies with the most toys wins.

    a. My family is more important than toys.

    b. I can't take it with me.

14. Debt scares me.

    a. Debt allowed me to buy a home.

    b. I know people who manage debt responsibly.

15. Never loan money to a relative.

    a. I want to help friends and relatives.

    b. I can be clear when a loan is really a gift in disguise.

16. I can control my children with money.

    a. I don't like being controlled by someone else.

    b. My parents didn't succeed in controlling me with money.

    c. I brought up my children to make good decisions.

17. Only I can handle the family's money right.

    a. I don't want that much responsibility.

    b. It's not all about me—it's about us.

    c. I want/need a partner in this.

18. I make too much money to ever change jobs.

    a. Stress can kill me, and then I'll really change jobs.

    b. My happiness is more important than money.

    c. My family would rather have me happy than rich.

19. Independent women handle their own money alone.

    a. Independence doesn't have to mean being alone and doing it alone.

    b. Collaborating doesn't take my independence away.

    c. Sharing doesn't take my independence away.

20. The world is abundant for everyone but me.

    a. We are all in this together.

    b. My journey is the perfect journey for me.

    c. God's schedule just might not be my schedule.

All these examples show how to find the truth behind those limiting beliefs—the ones that support not only your financial life but also your life in general.

Take your Restated Beliefs and answer these questions for each belief:

1.   Is it false?

2.   Is it affecting my life?

3.   Do I want to shift my behavior?

If the answer to any of the three questions is yes, you need to examine that belief further. Look for facts that discredit this belief. This is not the time to come up with what you *hope* to believe. This is where—without a doubt—you can say, "This is a fact; this is my truth." You need to embrace the fact and proclaim, "I believe this 100 percent."

 Work with each belief in your Restated Belief log. Write the facts you uncover in the spaces provided.

STEP THREE: RECREATE IT

You restated your unexamined beliefs and came up with evidence to debate their truth. Now let's recreate those beliefs to make them yours. What do I mean? As you discovered, these limiting beliefs—whether conscious or unconscious—stopped you from moving forward in your financial life because they were not your true beliefs. Now it's time to create new *growing edge* affirmations that support your visions.

> I don't know your experience with affirmations, but my experiences haven't always turned out the way I hoped—usually, because I reached too far. Just saying it didn't make it so. The Empowerment Institute's technique of working with the growing edge solved this problem for me. I know it will do the same for you.

Because you are so entrenched in your financial habits, it's important to possess affirmations that put you on your *growing edge*. The *growing edge* is the place where you feel energetically engaged in life. If you think of that garden again, your new financial beliefs act as the seeds in your garden of life. The growing edge is where the new plant breaks out of the seed cover—through the soil and into the sunlight. It's not the full flower in bloom but neither is it the seed itself. Likewise, your growing edge will gently push you into a new financial world.

The image of riding a wave is another way to think of the growing edge. The wave's greatest power is right at its leading edge. If you are in front of the wave, you crash and fall; but if you are too far behind, you slowly sink. When you are on that growing edge, you easily ride the wave the whole distance. That is exactly where you want to be when turning your old beliefs into new affirmations.

At the growing edge, you push yourself just enough to be a little uncomfortable—not so much that you doubt it will happen and not so little that you feel stagnant, standing in the same place; on the growing edge, you feel confident that growth will occur.

While you would like to go all the way to the *perfect* affirmation, you need to make sure it is believable (and doable). That *perfect* affirmation might push you too far (in the back of your mind, you may already be saying, "I hope I can do this, but I'm not really sure it's possible"). Instead, you need realistic affirmations that push you to your growing edge so you can confidently say, "Oh, yes, I can do this!"

> Do you remember Mary whose father taught her "without money, I am nothing"? The perfect affirmation would have been "my life is the same whether I have money or not." But growing up with a family that modeled her father's belief and living sixty years with her father's foundation, that perfect affirmation went too far. It wasn't something she really believed—yet. She needed to find an affirmation that would put her on her growing edge. "With or without money, my family loves me" was as far as she could go at first. She found evidence to support this, and although she felt some discomfort saying it, she could begin to believe it. This was the affirmation she could say *yes* to.

Your growing edge may not seem far enough at first, but remember you don't want to push too far just to crash and fall. Your growing edge needs to be realistic for where you exist today. Little by little, your growing edge will expand until you reach that perfect affirmation. Pushing too fast will only slow, stall, or stop the process entirely. But remember you still need to push enough to find that uncomfortable place where you feel growth blossoming.

From some of the examples mentioned earlier, here are the growing edge affirmations:

1. I trust myself to acquire the knowledge I need about money.
(I can't be trusted knowing about money.)

2. I pay cash for expenses under $100.
(I can avoid paying for things by manipulating money.)

3. With or without money, my family loves me.
(Without money, I am nothing.)

4. My basic goodness does not change.
(Good people don't have money—or money is dirty.)

5. I make good buying decisions by taking advantage of bargains.
(I am bad (or irresponsible) with money.)

6. I am successful because of my work ethic.
(I need an expensive education to be successful.)

7. I know what job makes me happy.
(I need a steady, reliable job at all costs.)

8. It is a privilege to work with me.
(I shouldn't be paid for helping people.)

9. I choose life over stress.
(There's no such thing as too much money.)

10. I have enough to take care of today.
(I will never have enough money for what I need.)

11. I keep track of my cash expenditures.
(Budgets don't work, especially for me.)

12. I deserve one $10 treat a week.
(Spending money on myself is frivolous.)

13. I enjoy the toys I now own.
(He who dies with the most toys wins.)

14. I am thankful for my home mortgage.
(Debt scares me.)

15. I can help my sister with a loan by communicating clear expectations.
(I should never loan money to a relative.)

16. I only help my children from generosity, not control.
(I can control my children with money.)

17. I review the family finances weekly with my wife.
(Only I can handle the family's money correctly.)

18. I prioritize what makes me happy.
(I make too much money to change jobs.)

19. I ask for assistance where and when needed.
(Independent women handle their own money alone.)

20. Every day I find examples of abundance in my life.
(The world is abundant for everyone but me.)

Of course, these are just examples. Each of us will have different growing edge affirmations. Only you can determine the affirmation that moves you forward on your journey.

G o back to your Restated Beliefs and Truth log in the back of the book. In your journal, create a growing edge affirmation for each belief. Follow these guidelines for writing an effective affirmation.

- Use clear, concise language.

- Employ positive language; avoid negatives.

- Utilize present tense as if you are already doing it.

- Keep it brief.

- Keep it simple.

When you think you have each growing edge affirmation, ask yourself these questions:

1. Does it push me too far?

2. Does it push me far enough?

3. Am I on that *uncomfortable* growing edge?

 Rework the affirmation until you have it just right. When you do, write it in the Growing Edge Affirmations section at the back of your book.

Chapter V

I CAN SEE CLEARLY NOW

Now you've built a real foundation under yourself. Your new growing edge affirmations provide you with the tools to make real change in your financial life. Now more conscious in thinking about money, you've uncovered beliefs that kept you stuck in old dysfunctional patterns. You examined the belief's veracity and recreated powerful new beliefs. Now you possess a fighting chance to make your financial visions real—your blindfold is off!

You can and will change your financial stories. When I first work with individuals and couples, they may feel frustrated because they want to start working on their *problems* immediately. For them, it seems like forever before they tackle the issues they first came to see me about. But without working on their underlying beliefs, I know any financial decisions they make to fix their problems will not last. They need the strong foundation of examined, true beliefs to give real change the chance to bloom.

Do you remember Jerry and Susan who were fraught with fear of owing more on their home than it was worth? They had all the facts down on paper as to why the numbers didn't work, why they were stuck, and why they would never get ahead. They knew there was no way out. We worked with their beliefs regarding taking care of themselves, responsibility for debt, and what was most important in their lives. Except for a few minutes at the beginning of each session to answer their questions about prioritizing debt payments, we didn't focus on their problems.

Yet, a year later, Jerry retired; they were out from under the burden of their house (without bankruptcy) and had moved to the place of their dreams. During a previous visualization exercise, they had both described their new home. Now they lived out their dream of that new home—faster than they ever expected and with much less work—or at least less *conventional* work! Believe me, I know analyzing beliefs involves work!

And Laurie and Joel, with a second child on the way, who handled finances separately? That baby arrived, they made it through maternity leave, and now have regular conversations—together—about financial decisions. Sure, there are still some difficulties, but they deal with them as a couple, not two individuals going it alone.

Sally, who was *bad at math*, is now fully engaged in making financial decisions for the family. And she no longer worries about being bad at math—she lets her husband do the quantifying of their financial life!

And best of all, Dan, the young twenty-year-old with a new career and too much debt. Here's an excerpt from a recent e-mail he sent me:

"I have made a significant reduction in my overall debt since your conference while also contributing substantially to my 401k. I can't thank you enough for the advice you shared. It has had a very real impact."

In all of these examples, we didn't tackle the problems head-on; we didn't stay mired in the money mess they found themselves in. Instead, we wrestled with those beliefs that were keeping them stuck in the same patterns over and over again, once again proving, *The Problem with Money? Is Not About the Money!*

So, like the people above, you've finished the hard work with your beliefs Now it's time to put your financial goals into place. Just like you did with your growing edge affirmation, you will move things forward by taking the next step—not all the steps—just the *next* step. Taking giant steps stymies you because the steps become much too large and too overwhelming.

Years ago, as a new, young professional, I decided to have a financial plan completed by an investment advisor to see what others in my field were doing. He asked me questions about what I wanted from retirement, how I would educate my children (at that point I had none), and what I wanted to leave when I died (Huh? I just started living!). I answered the questions as best as I could.

Along with some great advice, the finished plan told me to start saving $200 a month then—two years before my *proverbial* two children would be born—so I could pay for their college education! Now, no doubt, this was great advice, but somehow it seemed a bit much for someone who wasn't even married yet. Because of that plan's one giant step, I threw out the whole thing. It was just too overwhelming for me to even consider it.

It's important to be realistic about your goals and not push too far, too fast. As with your growing edge affirmations, you want growing edge goals. The visualizations you experienced gave you information about where you want to go. Now let's commit to the next steps to make those visions real.

First, choose just one area, maybe debt. If you grew up with an unrealistic belief about credit cards and find yourself with too much credit card debt, where do you even start? Looking at the results of your debt visualization, you might have recorded, "I want to stop relying on debt." But what will your next step be in moving toward that goal?

Remember the workshop I did for young twenty-somethings? Seth shared that he had more credit card debt than he wanted because he used his card for impulse purchases. His next step was to "only use his credit card for emergencies." But he confessed, "First, I need to pick it up at RiRa's where I left it for a bar tab!" After we finished laughing, we suggested maybe the next step is to define emergency.

Your spending plan vision might be to "have a spending plan." I think you can agree just that suggestion stops you in your tracks. Where do you start? What is the next step? I usually suggest by first quantifying what you spend now. You may have some spotty recorded information from the past, but usually because you've been avoiding the big **B**, you'll need to gather information. The next step might be to gather the last two month's spending to analyze where your money is going.

The vision and next step for abundance can sometimes be tricky. So it helps me (and may help you too) to think of abundance as another term for investment—investment in yourself and the belief that you deserve all that your life offers. As I mentioned before, beliefs about obtaining abundance can be misleading and tough—do you just sit back and wait for it? No, I believe you achieve abundance by being abundant with yourself. Your goal for abundance might be to put $100 a month into a savings account or retirement plan.

By just taking the next step toward each of your financial goals, you keep the journey interactive and fresh. You are free to adjust the process as you move toward the ultimate goal. As you accomplish each step, you not only gather new information for the following step, but more importantly, positively reinforce what you can accomplish. By working with just the next step—one at a time—you possess the freedom to keep your focus on today's step and your eyes on the ultimate prize. It's a process you can easily commit to.

In all seven areas, what is your next step for your Financial Vision? Remember you want just the next step—not the giant step. The next step might seem too tiny, but sometimes that tiny step can be the most difficult. Don't be embarrassed to write it down. Any positive movement forward is something to celebrate.

Use the Financial Visions and Next Steps worksheet at the back of your book to record the next step for all seven areas. Be clear with each step and make sure it is just the *next* step not the *perfect* step. (Although there is space to record future *next steps*, you only need to list one now.)

Next find a Growing Edge Affirmation that gives you the foundation to make that vision real. It might be one you've already found or you may need a new one. You have all the tools you need to find the right one to keep you moving on the path to real and lasting financial change.

 Record the Affirmation under the Next Step.

Chapter VI

FINANCIALLY CONSCIOUS

A s you may have guessed, this is not a static process. You won't go through this one time and call it quits. Because you are ever evolving, from time to time you will need to rework your affirmations and next steps to stay on your growing edge and move toward your financial vision.

This whole process is about living a *financially conscious* life—not unconscious, nor over-conscious. Our goal is to discover the right balance of living financially conscious. The examination of your beliefs showed you where you really want to be. Aware of your beliefs and values, you possess the tools to support the continuous living of a financially conscious life.

But how do you do that? By committing to some routine practices. If you have completed other self-help programs, you know this method works. Long-lasting change and new habits only happen when you personally commit to them.

To see the reality of your dreams, you need to commit to a plan, just like building a home. Following these steps below will make the commitment tangible:

1. Draw a blueprint for change.

2. Lay a strong foundation.

3. Structure it.

4. Personalize it.

5. Update it.

DRAW A BLUEPRINT FOR CHANGE

You have created the next steps for all seven areas of your financial life. Together these areas make up your money life so you will need to work with all of them to create real financial change. For example, you can't change your relationship with debt or abundance if you don't change your relationship with spending. One area influences the other; you must bind them together with a powerful financial vision—and a clear, concise plan. Remember, you are motivated to grow and change your finances by the power of your visions; articulating a plan strengthens your commitment.

xamine all seven areas of Next Steps. On your Financial Visions and Next Step worksheet, prioritize the seven areas by assigning them numbers one through seven with one being the most important and seven being the least important. Which area is most significant? Which is less essential? Is there a natural order to them? Prioritizing is imperative because although you want to stay focused on all seven factors, some days you may only be able to work with one.

With *My Blueprint for Change* in the back of the book, use clear concise words to write the seven Next Steps in order of importance. This is your financial blueprint for change—your own personal working plan. (You may also do this on a large sheet of paper to hang on your wall to remind you of your commitment to live a financially conscious life.)

Next, develop a realistic timeline for accomplishing each step of the plan. Remember, this timeline should also put you on your growing edge—not too fast, not too slow. In the right margin of the Blueprint, add the date you will accomplish each step.

Finally, at the bottom of your Blueprint, list the Required Resources needed to support you in your plan. Be specific. If necessary, speak with a professional for more information and additional resources. (You may need to add or adjust your Next Steps to accommodate this list.)

LAY A STRONG FOUNDATION

As you've learned, the foundation for a conscious financial life is your beliefs. You have exuded a Herculean effort by examining these beliefs to make them beliefs you can really believe in. You now have the opportunity to use those beliefs as a strong foundation for moving through financial change. These beliefs are the wind beneath your wings.

You've already examined your beliefs and turned them into growing edge affirmations. Yet now that you have your plan before you, you may have uncovered another limiting belief waiting to trip you up. If so, you have the tools to deal with it: *State It*, *Debate It*, and *Recreate It*. Make it your truth.

Review the Growing Edge Affirmations you listed on your Financial Vision and Next Step worksheet. Fine-tune them if necessary. Do they push you too far or perhaps not far enough? Are you on that *uncomfortable* growing edge?

Record the affirmations below each step of your Blueprint and modify them if necessary to fit with each prioritized next step.

Now, study the steps as a whole. Is there a general underlying belief to them? Is there a connecting theme? Find an overriding growing edge affirmation that is the foundation for your plan. Take the time to State It, Debate It, and Recreate It. Find the affirmation that best supports your overall plan.

 Write this in bold letters at the top and bottom of your Blueprint.

STRUCTURE IT

A house is only as strong as the structure itself. Your financial visions are no different. How will you spend time working on your plan? How will you fit this into your life? Anytime you add something new, something else has to give. You need to find the time and space for it.

You don't need much time, but you do need to be consistent. It's important to find time each day to remind yourself of your next steps and overall vision. Because you're establishing new habits in your life, you must develop routines with specific times and places to nourish your new plan and beliefs. As writer Annie Dillard said, "How we spend our days is, of course, how we spend our lives."

Consistency is crucial. Studies show it takes about a month for a new habit to form. If you dependably work on your plan, it will become a habit. Dedicate the same time each day for your plan—perhaps when you wake each morning. With a fresh mind, you can energize your day with your affirmations, fully conscious of what you want to accomplish. Bedtime (or meditation) is another obvious choice. You can use the power of your subconscious to make miracles happen!

Any time of the day—every day—is just right. You just need to find that time each day that allows you to be consistent and conscious.

Develop a detailed structure for working with your plan. Be specific; come up with as many details as possible for how it will work.

Commit to working with the plan at least once a day for thirty days and see how it feels. If you don't have a sense of what time of day is right for you, experiment until you find the right time— just remember—it must be at least once a day. If you remember that you are taking this time to move toward your new financial vision (leaving those problems behind), finding the time will be less difficult.

Answer these questions to help you develop the structure for your plan and decide on the specifics:

> How much time will I need?
>
> What time of day is best? Be specific even if it may change as you fine-tune.
>
> Where will I work with my plan? My office? My home? My bedroom? The kitchen? Where?
>
> When will I start?

 Under the *Required Resources* of your Blueprint, write your detailed and structured plan for being financially conscious.

At the end, sign your name to endorse your full commitment to your Blueprint for Change.

PERSONALIZE IT

Now let's use your creative side to strengthen your plan and foundational beliefs. Your creativity yields unlimited support for your visions. "Creativity is a type of learning process where the teacher and pupil are located in the same individual," according to British author Arthur Koestler. Creativity provides an opportunity to use the strengths of both teacher and pupil to advance your visions in fun and effective ways.

Creativity gives you direct access to the strength of your visions and commitment to change. With creativity, you can quickly access your plan with the strength of your conscious and subconscious mind. Do you remember the phrase, "Calgon, take me away?" Just hearing the words would transport you to an image of a luxurious bubble bath in a quiet, peaceful room. Younger folks who may not recognize the advertising slogan will need to trust me on this—the creative catalyst of that ad took most people right to the powerful vision.

What creative catalyst can you use? It can be anything—anything that speaks to your creative side. If you're aural, you can write and repeat anagrams, simple poems, or limericks. If you're visual, you can think of concrete images to remind you where you are going. If you love to sing (even if others don't like to hear you), write a simple song or change the words to a song you love. If you're an artist, draw it, paint it, photograph it, or sculpt it.

It can be as simple as feeling a smooth rock in your pocket or seeing sticky notes on your bathroom mirror or in your car. Your creative catalyst can be any personal form that triggers the memory of your financial vision.

Think about what creative form works best for you. What medium is natural to you? Don't say you have no creative side—everyone does!

And don't work too hard on finding the right form. Usually the first method to pop into your head is the right one. Your creativity is always willing and ready to serve on a moment's notice.

Once you decide on the form, take time to develop it. Getting lost in your creative process is a wonderful experience involving new insights and new depth. As a very important part of your journey, ensure you give it the time it is due. Play with it and have fun.

No right or wrong exists when it comes to your own creativity. Just remember your creative catalyst only needs to remind you—and no one else—of your overall goal and vision.

 Put your creative catalyst under the *Structure* section on your Blueprint. Because this is truly your own personal form—you will know best how to represent it. Most importantly, have it accessible to you each day as you work with your Blueprint.

UPDATE IT

Like any home, it's important to update and repair your plan, especially since you're working with only your next step and growing edge affirmation. Some steps you will accomplish quickly, but some will require more time. You need to constantly update or replace steps to keep traveling on your growing edge and moving toward your vision.

Are you increasingly discouraged with your plan? Does it feel stagnant with no movement? Have you pushed yourself too far and feel it's impossible? Or maybe you haven't push yourself far enough and you're bored. Time to *State It*, *Debate It*, and *Recreate It*. Rework that next step and affirmation to return to your growing edge. Repair and update—there's nothing to be ashamed of—it's just time to regroup.

Maybe you've accomplished that next step, and it's time to find a new next step to continue moving forward. You have the tools to keep moving on your journey to financial change.

Remember these processes are personal. No one can tell you how to do it. Only you can decide what works best. You just need to remember to stay on your growing edge—that place where your financial dreams break through the soil on their way to blossoming. As long as you are on that edge, you are growing!

Finally, it is important not to do this alone.

I remember *surviving* the renovation of our home. It was long and painful—much longer than expected. The vision of the finished rooms with more sunlight, bright new paint, and gleaming hardwood floors kept us slogging through the sawdust, early-morning hammering, and loss of privacy. But some days even that didn't seem enough. The support of friends and family with beliefs in our vision and enthusiasm for the finished product kept us going through the difficult months.

Ask someone to be with you on this journey—someone to report your progress to or even journey with. Author Pearl S. Buck said, "The person who tries to live alone will not succeed as a human being. His heart withers if it does not answer another heart. His mind shrinks away if he hears only the echoes of his own thoughts and finds no other inspiration." Don't go it alone; share your journey with someone.

Make a regular plan to devote extra time (outside of your daily commitment to make it a habit) to update and refresh your Blueprint. How will you know when it is time to update? Typically, you should evaluate your plan each time you finish a next step or at least every two or three weeks.

How will you work with your plan to keep it fresh and up to date? Because your Blueprint is a working document, add or subtract things as needed. You'll be able to tell you're working it by the changes and updates you make.

Add a pre-established date when you will do your first in-depth evaluation and update. Add this date to your Blueprint under your Creative Catalyst.

Remember a time will come when you will need to draw up a completely new Blueprint. The good news? This means you've made major positive changes in your financial life!

Lastly, whom will you discuss your progress (and challenges) with? Who will support you on this journey?

 Contact them now and ask them to join you on this important journey. Perhaps, you can even work through the book together. How can they help you along and hold you accountable? Do you need set meetings, perhaps weekly, monthly, or quarterly? Finally, ask them to endorse your plan by signing below your signature on *My Blueprint for Change.*

Chapter VII

TAKING IT TO THE WORLD

ongratulations! You are on your way to living a financially conscious life. You examined your money beliefs and recreated them to give you a foundation for making long-lasting, real change. You identified next steps on your path and drew up a Blueprint for Change with structure and plans for building your new life with money. You have resources and support to sustain you on your journey.

But it doesn't stop here. This Blueprint for Change will affect other parts of your life—family, relationships, work, and much more. You have a new sense of capability and responsibility; your overall attitude toward life has actually shifted.

Because money exists all around you, leading a financially conscious life will shape everyone and everything—everywhere! Your *old* money life led you into patterns and situations that didn't reflect your true beliefs. Living a financially conscious life supported by your own *examined* money beliefs will now shore up who you truly are.

Henry David Thoreau said, "Things do not change; we change." This process has entailed deep-level transformation with not only change in doing—but change in being. How you are with money has changed—not what you do with money. Let me say that again. How you *are* with money has changed—not what you *do* with money. Being, not doing, makes all the difference.

Leading a financially conscious life and being your true self puts you firmly on a path of change. When you change, the world changes. Your personal money beliefs and values will shift your economic world. And with this process, everyone becomes a facilitator of economic change in our world.

Why is economic change so important? For years, society has been hurtling forward, gathering speed as it accumulates more and more things. Acquisitions grew bigger and bigger. Our thirst and hunger for more and more couldn't be quenched. There was always a new gadget, a better gizmo, a bigger car, a larger house. Consumerism and credit grew to where we could not be satiated.

We acquired more and more debt and we bought into the idea that we were only as good as our possessions. As we burdened ourselves with this easy debt, we found ourselves in vicious cycles of needing more debt to continue the lifestyles we created.

Or, maybe we cowered in fear as we watched the world spin out of control. We didn't like what was going on, and we weren't going to join in and add to the problems, but we didn't do anything to improve the chaos either. Our unexamined beliefs kept us talking about *them—those other people*. As long as it was about *others*, we accepted no responsibility. Stuck in dysfunctional money beliefs, we watched the collapse happen.

Everyone watched as the world was built around the almighty dollar. We tied our worth to our wealth, believing our country was powerful because of our riches. Now those riches have eroded. You and I know the future is at the mercy of new economic times. But can we shift that box a little? Can we look at it in another way?

I believe we face this economic crisis in order to re-evaluate who we are in relationship to money. Who am I without money, without possessions, and without accumulation? In these economic times, I believe we must stop, reflect, and change course. It's our chance for growth and even gratitude.

When we find ourselves in a place where money is no longer enough we must reexamine our standards for real value. Do we find value in terms of what we do and what we own? Do we find our own worth by comparing ourselves to our friends and neighbors? Is value determined by how much we earn and what we'll have when we retire? Is the accumulation of bigger and better goods and larger bank accounts the barometer of our importance? What and where is our worth—both individually and as a society?

Your work in this book entailed examining your money beliefs and making them truly yours. "Believe only what you yourself test and judge to be true," Buddha said. You have tested your money beliefs and recreated them to make them your own. Now you can define real value in your life—without blinders or blindfolds.

I believe we face these economic times for just that reason—to examine our beliefs and find real value in our lives. Losing sight of what fed our souls, we blindly pursued consumerism at the expense of our freedom to choose. We bought into today's economic times because we tried to put value in our lives with things rather than each other.

It's not about working longer and harder for the sake of buying the latest and greatest consumer product. It's not about the size of our retirement account when our health may not see us to retirement. And it's not about the size of our cars or homes when we live in lonely isolation from our neighbors and community. We each have a choice.

Challenging economic times involve finding a new path—a new power in the world—an alternative to the powerful dollar. We all lost sight of the initial purpose of money. Instead of giving it economic power for the exchange of goods and services, we increased its value as a substitute for the real intangible values of life—each other, our families, and our communities. But you can change that.

Through this book, you've debated those beliefs and recreated them to reflect your real, intangible values. Now you can use money, this man-made resource, to put real value into your life. You can ask, "How do I find value in my life—does this add or subtract from what is truly important to me?" Now you can answer with your real personal values and not those of the society and world.

When I work with people in my money coaching and workshops, they are often surprised to discover what they value most doesn't require a lot of money.

> A woman frantic with financial worry about retirement in three years discovers she loves her work, doesn't need or want to retire, and the retirement she ultimately sees for herself doesn't require the accumulation of great wealth—only her gardens and family around her.

Conversely, those with great wealth usually discover that having riches doesn't make a difference if there is no health, peace of mind, or acceptance of their abundance in non-monetary things. Money is just the illusion of value in their lives, and not surprisingly, there is *never enough* to fill them up.

I like to dream that in challenging economic times we will all find our way back to real value—the value of ourselves and those we connect with.

> Recently, my husband and I were at a restaurant sitting across from a mother and her eight-year-old daughter. While her mother text messaged, the daughter sat dejected and alone. The mother took a break to place the order and commented to the server that they were celebrating her daughter's report card. Then she picked up the phone again and called a friend to talk about shopping. The whole time they waited for their food, she was on the phone while her daughter sat quietly waiting for acknowledgement.

This change to discover real value starts with you. How much better for everyone (including my husband and me) if the mother had really been with her daughter—not only in body but also in spirit—if there had been a real connection between them, if she had given her the gift of time and presence—not just the gift of doing. This is the kind of value I'm referring to.

Can we find value in children playing in the great outdoors, climbing trees, building forts, and discovering the wonders of nature instead of buying them expensive computers, game systems, or large-screen TVs? Can we find worth in inviting friends over for dinner rather than having an expensive night out? Instead of seeing value in the mansion down the road or bigger and better things, can we find importance in the eyes of our loved ones and our communities?

Instead of putting in long hours *to get ahead*, can we put those hours into building a stronger family, community, or world? Instead of thinking *they* need to fix it, can we find value in being part of the solution—without pay? Can we take pride in that lost concept—*civic duty*?

In these economic times, I hope you will uncover the truths of your personal beliefs and redefine where you really find value—in each other—not things. Mahatma Gandhi said, "You must be the change you want to see in the world."

My dream is that this book will be the catalyst spurring the discovery of your personal beliefs and the redefinition of your values. Doing so will change the way you think about money. And in turn, the way we all think about our world.

Thank you for joining me in that dream!

WORKSHEET SECTION

The following section includes the worksheets that will facilitate your journey of becoming financially conscious. Earlier sections of the book clearly explain how to employ each of the following worksheets:

- Unexamined Beliefs

- Restated Beliefs and Truths

- Growing Edge Affirmations

- Financial Visions and Next Steps

- Blueprint for Change

The final goals of the exercises are to (1) identify unexamined financial beliefs, (2) create and claim your own monetary truths, (3) formulate growing edge affirmation to spur financial change, (4) construct your own financial vision, and (5) lay out the steps needed to implement that financial change. Ultimately, I hope that you will grow financially conscious of your beliefs about true worth and value, and radically change the way you view the world and how you interact in it.

UNEXAMINED BELIEFS

1. _____
   _____

2. _____
   _____

3. _____
   _____

4. _____
   _____

5. _____
   _____

6. _____
   _____

7. _____
   _____

8. _____
   _____

9. _____
   _____

10. _____
    _____

RESTATED BELIEFS AND TRUTHS

1. _____

    a. _____

    b. _____

    c. _____

2. _____

    a. _____

    b. _____

    c. _____

3. _____

    a. _____

    b. _____

    c. _____

4. _____

    a. _____

    b. _____

    c. _____

5. _____

    a. _____

    b. _____

    c. _____

6. _____

   a. _____

   b. _____

   c. _____

7. _____

   a. _____

   b. _____

   c. _____

8. _____

   a. _____

   b. _____

   c. _____

9. _____

   a. _____

   b. _____

   c. _____

10. _____

   a. _____

   b. _____

   c. _____

GROWING EDGE AFFIRMATIONS

1. _____

2. _____

3. _____

4. _____

5. _____

6. _____

7. _____

8. _____

9. _____

10. _____

FINANCIAL VISIONS AND NEXT STEPS

1. Overall Attitude: _____

_____

Next Step: _____

Next Step: _____

Next Step: _____

Growing Edge Affirmation: _____

2. Financial Ability/Responsibility: _____

_____

Next Step: _____

Next Step: _____

Next Step: _____

Growing Edge Affirmation: _____

3. Personal Spending: _____

_____

Next Step: _____

Next Step: _____

Next Step: _____

Growing Edge Affirmation: _____

4. Access to Credit and Debt: _____

_____

Next Step: _____

Next Step: _____

Next Step: _____

Growing Edge Affirmation: _____

5. Relationships: _____

_____

Next Step: _____

Next Step: _____

Next Step: _____

Growing Edge Affirmation: _____

6. Work: _____

Next Step: _____

Next Step: _____

Next Step: _____

Growing Edge Affirmation: _____

7. Abundance: _____

_____

Next Step: _____

Next Step: _____

Next Step: _____

Growing Edge Affirmation: _____

BLUEPRINT FOR CHANGE

Overall Affirmation: _____

NEXT STEPS

1. _____

Affirmation: _____

2. _____

Affirmation: _____

3. _____

Affirmation: _____

4. _____

Affirmation: _____

5. _____

Affirmation: _____

6. _____

Affirmation: _____

7. _____

Affirmation: _____

REQUIRED RESOURCES

1. _____

2. _____

3. _____

STRUCTURE

What: _____

Where: _____

When: _____

Creative Catalyst: _____

Date to Renovate: _____

Overall Affirmation: _____

Signature of Commitment: _____

Endorsement: _____

ACKNOWLEDGMENTS

This journey has been such a long one, that to thank everyone along the way would be another whole book. Yet, there are a few people who require special treatment.

First to all of you—friends, colleagues or clients who said *finally* to this step of my journey, thank you for your patience in helping me find my voice and my courage. It was a long time coming, but your encouragement has been priceless. You all know who you are—I couldn't have done it without you.

To all the teachers who helped me on my personal journey—you have been an inspiration in so many ways. The dedication to your life's purpose and your deep passion for sharing with others has given me the tools for doing the same for others. Your work has modeled creativity, dedication and strength of purpose. Thank you for sharing it with me.

A special thank you to all the clients who shared their financial lives (and tax returns) with me over these many years. You're more than just clients; you're friends who have helped me discover the lessons you find in this book and much, much more. You've made my life as an accountant so much more than numbers.

To my accounting and financial colleagues, both at Honeck-O'Toole and other related financial and business services: deep gratitude for the support you've given me in providing impeccable service to our deserving clients. It's been a joy to work as a team in helping people wade through this complicated tax and financial world we live in.

To Ellen Reid and her team who helped me through the publishing process; thanks for hanging in there when my analytical mind tangled with your creativity. I know it wasn't easy, but eventually I came around and my creative side put the analytical one to rest. Your coaching, mentoring and hard work culminated in a beautiful book I am proud of. I hope you are too.

A giant thank you to my family. To my mother and four sisters—you're always there to support your quirky sister Jane, to my three sons—I hope this inspires you to follow your dreams, and to my four step-children, their partners and seven step-grandchildren—never in my life did I expect such a rich, full and accepting family—thanks for opening your arms to me.

And, last but not least, love and thanks to my husband Wayne. I know my new and crazy ideas haven't made for an easy ride, but it's so much easier knowing you're at my side. As you once told me, *we can do anything—we're Wayne and Jane!*

That says it all.

HOW TO ENGAGE
THE AUTHOR

Jane Honeck, CPA, PFS author, speaker, and seminar leader is available to help you further discover *The Problem with Money? Is Not About the Money!* Jane's coaching, workshops and presentations use her insightful knowledge of the intricate web of money beliefs, along with her years of expertise as an accountant, to lead you and/or your organization to a whole new life with money.

For more information contact:

Jane Honeck
50 Portland Pier
Portland, Me 04101
207-774-0882

Jane@janehoneck.com
www.janehoneck.com